"The pages of *Catastrop*
dramatic crises in the lives of
cussed in systematic detail in
cal meaning of servant leadership. Without any doubt this is the leadership style of
Jesus and one that He passed on to His disciples.

"Every believer will be challenged, inspired, and motivated through these pages
to be the servant leader he was saved to become!"

Jimmy Draper
President Emeritus, LifeWay Christian Resources

"Particularly thoughtful, inspiring, and useful, *Catastrophic Crisis* balances
sound research with case studies to bring seminary students and lifelong pastors
to the crucible that is ministerial leadership. For those who have yet to be in crisis, read this book in preparation, and for those of you who are in or have come
through a crisis, use this book to gain wisdom through reflection."

David G. Forney
Former Associate Dean of Faculty, Columbia Seminary; Editor, *Journal of Religious
Leadership*; and Pastor, First Presbyterian Church, Clarksville, Tennessee

"The Lord gave me the gift of encouragement/exhortation. As a result, when I
read those who write in this area to encourage those who have experienced pain and
gone through difficult times, it really resonates with my heart. You will be greatly
blessed by this book, *Catastrophic Crisis*, as the message unfolds to encourage you
in life's challenges."

Johnny Hunt
Former President, Southern Baptist Convention

"Do you think you are the only Christian leader who has faced a crisis in ministry? Think again! Better yet, read this book by my friend, Steve Echols, and co-author,
Allen England. This is a real-life case-study approach to some of the most difficult
circumstances in ministry. This book will both challenge and comfort you.

Rick Lance
Executive Director of the Alabama Baptist State Convention

"God leaves His fingerprints upon the crises of our lives so that by prayer and humility we may prove that His grace is sufficient. Steve Echols and Allen England have given us a profoundly practical analysis of the cruciality of leadership during seasons of catastrophe. Their insights offer hope and direction to church leaders everywhere who realize that the unexpected can happen to anyone at anytime. Read this book eagerly. Let the lessons seep deeply."

Dean Register
Founding Pastor, Crosspoint Community Church, Hattiesburg, Mississippi, and former President, Mississippi Baptist Convention

"Some life lessons are only learned in pain. This book provides a manual to help navigate the difficult waters of crisis. I commend it to you. The stories and principles will encourage and equip you for the journey of persistence in ministry leadership."

Ted H. Traylor
Pastor, Olive Baptist Church, Pensacola, Florida

"One of the most effective ways to learn is to learn from the experiences of others. In this helpful book, Steve Echols and Allen England take leaders to school on the experiences of real leaders managing real crises. The success of one's leadership often hangs on his ability to manage crises well. Learn how through this set of very interesting case studies."

J. Robert White
Executive Director, Georgia Baptist Convention

"In *Catastrophic Crisis*, Steve and Allen offer solid, biblical, practical advice for leading through a crisis. Their use of case studies in examining and applying the traits of good leadership captures the reader and drives home the sobering need to be prepared for leading through the tough circumstances—as well as the good ones."

Bryant Wright
President of the Southern Baptist Convention, and Senior Pastor, Johnson Ferry Baptist Church, Marietta, Georgia

Steve Echols
Allen England

Catastrophic
CRISIS

Ministry Leadership in the
Midst of Trial and Tragedy

ACADEMIC

NASHVILLE, TENNESSEE

Catastrophic Crisis:
Ministry Leadership in the Midst of Trial and Tragedy

Copyright © 2011 by Steve Echols and Allen England

ISBN: 978-0-8054-4976-1

Published by B&H Publishing Group
Nashville, Tennessee

Dewey Decimal Classification: 303.3
Subject Heading: LEADERSHIP \ DISASTERS \ CRISIS MANAGEMENT-
-CASE STUDIES

Unless otherwise indicated, Scripture quotations are from the *Holman Christian Standard Bible* ® Copyright © 1999, 2000, 2002, 2003, 2009 by Holman Bible Publishers. Used by permission.

Scripture citations marked NASB are from the New American Standard Bible. ©The Lockman Foundation, 1960, 1962, 1968, 1971, 1973, 1975, 1977. Used by permission.

Printed in the United States of America

1 2 3 4 5 6 7 8 9 10 11 12 • 17 16 15 14 13 12 11
R

We wish to dedicate this volume
to our wives Julie (Steve) and Jane (Allen)
for their incredible encouragement and support through the years.
This book is just the latest evidence of their continued blessings
upon our lives and ministries.

We also dedicate this to our children, Jeremy and Joy (Steve), and
Wil and Luke (Allen), and to our students as the
next generation of Christian leaders.

Above all, we dedicate this book and our efforts in leadership studies
to our Lord and Savior Jesus Christ.

Contents

Part II: The Crushing Unexpected

Part III: Help and Hope

Foreword

Leadership is always challenging, but there are certain times when leadership is even more challenging than normal, especially during trial, suffering, and setback. The important and helpful book that you hold in your hands contains powerful leadership lessons learned at key times in the midst of real-life experiences, lessons that are often beyond our ability to fully grasp in the moment. Usually, it is only on reflection that these lessons can be communicated to others. The chapters in this book communicate those reflections in ways that we hope will provide guidance and instruction for others when their moments of challenge arise. The authors of this project, Allen England and Steve Echols, are to be commended for their vision and desire to provide such a useful resource.

In his book *The Problem of Pain,* C. S. Lewis says that God often uses the experiences of suffering as a megaphone to awaken us. According to Lewis, suffering and pain are often the essential means by which God brings about dependence, fortitude, patience, and forgiveness in His children, while also arousing acts of mercy and compassion among others. On February 5, 2008, the campus of Union University, where I serve as president, suffered massive damages from an EF-4 tornado. Bringing destruction to almost all aspects of our residential area and to several other key buildings on campus, the $45 million hit has been declared one of the worst disasters in Southern Baptist history. That morning we had over 3300 students in class, and nearly one-half of them were on campus when the tornado arrived at 7:02 that Tuesday evening—a night that we will never forget. That night we took 51 students to the hospital. Almost a dozen were seriously injured, and a few had lengthy hospital stays. Everyone who saw the campus during the first 48 hours was overwhelmed by the fact that the lives of all of the students who were on campus on that Tuesday evening were spared. For God's providential protection we remain grateful.

I was in my office with two other deans when the tornado struck the campus. We were able to get to the residential area of the campus within minutes after it touched down. The devastation was far greater than anything I could have imagined. After spending time with students trying to give direction and assurance, I spent the next six hours in the command center that evening communicating with everyone involved. When we returned to the campus about 2:00 a.m., I couldn't believe what I saw.

That picture of devastation was even more difficult to believe when the sun came up the next morning. The local, regional, and national media were all on campus early that Wednesday morning. After spending time with the media, we immediately began our initial assessment. We mapped out a five-step plan to get us through the initial 48-hour emergency period and then to move forward. The time invested on that Wednesday with campus leaders was critical, and the overarching five-stage plan served us well for the next several months. In many ways, those were the most critical moments of leadership that I had ever faced. Literally hundreds of decisions needed to be made. We needed wisdom; we needed God's help; we needed a framework for our plan; and we needed the Lord to provide agents of mercy for our time of need.

During this time we saw God's hand at work in answering our prayers. We witnessed thousands of acts of mercy and compassion from people who responded to the massive needs associated with Union University. These acts of mercy and compassion came from people near to the university and from people far away who knew hardly anything about Union University. Somehow the disastrous effects of the tornado touched the hearts of these many, many people who helped us through those difficult months. We are thankful for them, but most of all we are grateful for God's good and amazing providence and for the gift of hope that He provided for us. God's providence and the sense of hope were not only gifts to sustain us through those days; they were also the means that God used to give us the framework to begin to provide the guidance and leadership needed for our campus during this time of extreme need and challenge.

Christians have historically confessed that God as Father reigns with providential care over His universe, His creatures, and the flow of the stream of human history according to the purposes of His grace. The providence of God provides the best framework for all Christ followers and especially for Christian leaders to interpret the accounts shared in this book, including the account of the tornado that devastated large portions of the Union University campus. For me, providence moved from an abstract theological concept to being the very source of strength and direction needed for that critical hour.

The lives of those who have contributed to this book, like my own, will likely never be the same after experiencing the events portrayed in the chapters that follow. I know that my life will never be the same on this side of February 5, 2008. The events of that night will be etched in my memory for years to come and will continue to shape my understanding of leadership on a day-to-day basis. I will never forget the eerie darkness, the loud sound of the swirling tornado, the initial phone call telling me that portions of the campus had been hit, the first impressions after seeing the wall crumbling down, the look on the faces of the shocked students, and the amazing efforts of the rescue workers who were involved that night in the initial response. But most of all, I will never forget the sense of hope that carried us through that night and the many days thereafter.

I am deeply grateful for the privilege to write the foreword for this fine book, but in this brief section I cannot trace the details of all the events that have taken place over the past two years in response to that night of devastation. I can, however, testify to the reality that we often found ourselves in uncharted waters, functioning in an essentialist mode. Our entire leadership team continued to press on with hopefulness in God's good providence, with an assurance that the same providential God who protected us on that evening would provide for us and guide us along the way in the new journey that was now ours. Hope in God's goodness, in His grace, and in His providence has indeed carried us through the challenges of recent months.

Hope is a powerful word—a driving force in life. Hope includes a desire for something, but it is even more than that. It is an eager, confident expectation that sustains us while we work diligently and wait patiently. Hope is not escapism; it is an energizing motivation for faithful living in the here and now, especially for those in key leadership roles. In the midst of these challenges, hope serves to stabilize our lives as an anchor to link us to God's faithful providence. I think it would likely be the testimony of every contributor to this volume that hope shaped and directed their service and gave it motivation so that—while waiting in the midst of the trial or challenge—they were able to navigate their way forward with the assurance of God's guidance. Even for those whose situations may have turned out different from ours, it is now the power of hope in God's good providence that can begin to help shape the days to come. Leaders cannot function without an abiding sense of hopefulness in the providence of God.

This kind of hope is not self-reliant motivation, but a confidence in a God who intervenes in the affairs of human history. Without such a trust in the triune God, we would all have found the challenges such as those that are described in this book to be insurmountable. Leaders move forward in the midst of these times with the full recognition that God's providence transcends the experiences of men and women. In so doing, God can take actions that seem bad and use them for His good (Gen 50:20).

These challenges call for us to have a new mind-set, a new attitude, and a new spiritual framework to navigate our way. But like the people of God who have gone before us, we can allow these challenges to become instruments of transforming grace in our lives because we recognize that there is one overarching longing and purpose in life, and only God can make known that purpose and satisfy that longing. In the midst of the kinds of challenges and setbacks described by the contributors to this book, there will likely be times when haunting and perplexing questions spring up in our hearts. During those times it is often hard to see our way clearly, and it is often difficult to sing the hymns, to pray, or even to read Scripture. When that happens, what should Christ followers do? What should leaders do? Assume that God has abandoned us, that He does not care for us or does not love us? Assume that He is unable to help us? I think not. It is in these moments that we learn in new ways to trust the providence of God, even when we have unanswered questions. It is during these times that we are driven afresh to believe the truth of God's

Word, and ultimately to find rest in the great faithfulness of the one, true, and living God, who has made Himself known to us in Jesus Christ (John 1:18). It is my prayer that, as you work through the pages of this book, you will be encouraged to seek God afresh and in these times of reflection you will find strength, guidance, peace, and hope for the leadership calling that is yours. It is a joy to recommend to you this book and the life lessons regarding leadership that are communicated herein. I pray that this resource will be an instrument of grace for you in the days to come.

David S. Dockery
President, Union University
May 3, 2010

Acknowledgments

We are grateful to the following for their invaluable assistance in giving many hours to this book:

Teresa Golden for transcribing the interviews, securing the pictures for the case studies, and handling much of the correspondence; Karla McGehee for making corrections and formatting the manuscript; Charles Owusu for assisting in transcribing the interviews; Bill McClanahan for proofreading and giving us valuable input from a layman's perspective concerning the ministerial leadership in the case studies; and Dr. Dwayne McCrary and Pam Cole for their extensive help in proofreading and editing the document. Their assistance was extremely helpful in revising the material into a clearer and more readable format.

Steve is grateful for the support of Elizabeth Baptist Church, where he serves as bivocational pastor, which allowed him time off to complete this book.

We both appreciate the time for research and writing allowed to us by New Orleans Baptist Theological Seminary.

We are especially grateful for all the individuals who so graciously allowed us to tell their stories. In some instances, they shared these stories in the midst of tears and ongoing pain from these catastrophic crises. Their courage and faith inspired us and taught us much about leadership.

Introduction

*"Now we have this treasure in clay jars, so that this extraor-
dinary power may be from God and not from us. We are
pressured in every way but not crushed; we are perplexed
but not in despair; we are persecuted but not abandoned; we
are struck down but not destroyed."*   2 Corinthians 4:7–9

The Importance of Leadership Studies

As seminary professors, we encounter a variety of students when we teach
leadership courses. The vast majority of them realize the importance of
the subject in the practical world of vocational ministry. Yet inevitably,
a few students consider leadership studies a waste of time. They prefer
to study only the classical seminary curriculum courses. Both of us have
been amused when some in this latter group of students have sought us
later, sometimes desperately seeking leadership advice. Thankfully, serious errors in doctrinal or biblical interpretations are seldom the cause for
major problems in ministry in Southern Baptist churches. Unfortunately,
this is not the case with leadership issues. Leadership problems are the
leading cause of forced termination in Southern Baptist churches, and
the fallout has devastating effects on both the minister and the church.

1

This reality makes the study of leadership important, not only in seminary curriculums, but for the church in general.

The church is not alone in the quest for knowledge of how to lead successfully. The study of leadership has been of consuming interest both inside and outside the church. One reason for the current intense interest in leadership is the increasing complexity of the decisions leaders face. Leadership in ministry is no exception. Peter Drucker considered the job of being a senior pastor of a large church to be one of the four most difficult jobs in America.[1] Yet smaller churches are hardly the exception in regard to demand. Churches of all sizes have multiplied their ministries and programs. Churches tend to be more diverse in congregational makeup as well as in their target audiences. Often this plurality contributes to lack of consensus within the congregation. Consequently, ministerial leaders now face far less certainty in the outcomes of their decisions.

In addition to increased complexity, today's leaders have been forced to deal with change at a quickened pace. Along with communication, leadership theorists have identified change agency as a central function, if not the key function, of leadership. Robert Banks and Bernice Ledbetter observed that there is an increased interest in leadership "during periods of widespread uncertainty and change."[2] Even before the information age had fully blossomed, Daryl Conner opined that "never has so much changed so fast and with such dramatic implications for our entire world."[3] Now in the second decade of the twenty-first century, the pace of change is at warp speed. Programs in churches have an increasingly short shelf life. Congregations and communities are changing more rapidly than ever. Ministry leaders as well as secular leaders are searching for answers as to how to manage the tsunami of change.

Another cause for the intense interest in leadership is the number of visible leadership failures. Further addressing the heightened attention given to leadership, Banks and Ledbetter noted, "This is especially the case when they are public figures of whom people have considerable expectations or on whose performance much depends."[4] Failures in leadership are nothing new, but the informational age has made them much more public. Likewise, a number of high-profile failures in ministerial leadership in recent years have served as unfortunate examples of this tendency. These failures, especially those based on moral and ethical issues, have led not only to skepticism but also to a search for strategies to safeguard the integrity of leaders.

Closely akin to the failure of leadership, the angst of being in a perpetual crisis mode also has resulted in an increased focus on leadership. In society as a whole, whether certain challenges are truly crises is subject to debate. Yet the perception is often that they are. Again, the connectivity resulting from the information age could be a factor in encouraging this sense of crisis. However, the crises the church faces today are often not the result of an anxious environment. Examples of true crises in the church abound, including a declining church in Western developed nations and a severely persecuted church in many unreached portions of the earth.

Despite the increased urgency, the search for leadership concepts and practices to improve understanding and outcomes has fallen short. In recent decades, a proliferation of publications, consultancies, and academic curricula has occurred. Unfortunately, the increase of study and resources has not produced a consensus as to what constitutes effective leadership. Academic research has failed to find the "silver bullet" of leadership. One group of prominent scholars summarized, "For the last twenty years, the topic of leadership has become popular among scholars. . . . However, there remains no comprehensive understanding of what leadership is, nor is there an agreement among different theorists on what good or effective leadership should be."[5]

> *Academic research has failed to find the "silver bullet" of leadership.*

With the aforementioned factors, twenty-first century leaders face a formidable challenge in attempting to find the optimum approach. Often a prognosis for the results of a leadership style used by a specific leader in a particular leadership moment would seem as abysmally inaccurate as the local weather forecast. The difficulty of discerning the effect of a seemingly incalculable number of contextual factors contributes to the lack of consensus in leadership theory. However, the challenges that hinder universality in leadership theory and praxis need not prevent the discovery of best approaches for beneficial leadership outcomes. Simply put, the lack of an all-encompassing, unified theory of leadership does not preclude the potential effectiveness of certain leadership principles.

The Use of Crisis Case Studies for Leadership Lessons

One effective approach for finding helpful leadership practices is to study leadership in the midst of crisis. Bill George noted, "There is nothing quite like a crisis to test your leadership. It will make or break you as a leader."[6] The presence of a crisis event or circumstance intensifies the leadership challenge and spotlights the leader and the leadership moment. Crises accentuate the dynamics of leadership and reveal a leader's strengths and weaknesses in a way that ordinary challenges do not. For this reason, we utilized case studies of various crises in ministry as a means for understanding aspects of both favorable and unfavorable leadership practices.

> *"There is nothing quite like a crisis to test your leadership. It will make or break you as a leader."*

Like emergency drills, case studies serve as vehicles for advance preparation. These exercises are opportunities to hone skills and identify deficiencies. The desired outcome of such rehearsals is to make a positive difference when an actual emergency occurs. Thus, we hope reading these case studies will prepare leaders to face challenges in times of crisis. In addition, we note important principles concerning leadership in general and apply them to leadership praxis, particularly in the ministry context.

The case studies in this book represent leaders who faced a special kind of crisis. Leaders continually encounter challenges of all types. It is sometimes difficult to distinguish events that represent the ongoing nature of a leader's responsibility from true crises. What one leader might label a crisis, another leader perhaps would perceive as a routine difficulty of leadership. Depending on their skill level and the specific context, different leaders might consider similar events or circumstances to be on a scale from somewhat difficult to devastating. Therefore, an objective standard is required to discern the level of the challenge.

Herman Leonard observed a distinct difference between high-stakes situations and crises. Many organizations routinely deal with decisions that have important consequences. Ministry is certainly in that category. The potential for positive or negative effects of a ministry on its constituents is sobering to consider. Most ministries have high stakes in the potential outcome. Yet, according to Leonard, crises are more than the normal consequence of the actions of a leader or organization, no matter how significant the outcome may be. Crises "also have high variability, high contingency, urgency, and unplanned or accidental or unforeseeable elements, in such a form or combination that the routine application of existing routines will not be adequate to produce effective or acceptable performance or outcomes."[7] Leonard further proposed that a crisis "requires a substantially greater degree of adaptation and improvisation to deal with an essentially new situation and, therefore, constitutes a significantly different challenge of leadership."[8] The case studies we selected are out of the routine, even the routine of high pressure. They required a response from the leaders and their constituents that met the kinds of conditions that Leonard noted. But we added a further delineation.

In titling the book *Catastrophic Crisis*, we deliberately upped the stakes. We did not choose the word *catastrophic* lightly. The etymology of *catastrophic* is from the Greek *katastrophē*, which means "ruin" or "destruction." It is from the verb form meaning "to overturn."[9] In other words, a catastrophic crisis is something that turns the world upside-down and forever alters the leadership landscape. We felt that this term describes the events that occurred in these case studies and situations like them. Leaders may face a number of crises in their tenures, but a catastrophic crisis may occur once in a lifetime. Some leaders may never experience an event of this magnitude. However, the lessons they can learn from those who have endured such crises are applicable to leadership in general.

The ministry settings that we chose had circumstances in which the normative method of operation was no longer possible. The context in which leadership took place was turned upside down. For the most part, the leader could not have anticipated the situation. Part One concerns cataclysmic events. Of these, two relate to catastrophic damage inflicted by horrific weather. Another incident involves an accidental tragedy of horrendous consequence. Two more situations resulted from individuals outside the congregation inflicting a catastrophe on the churches. In one instance, it was a violent act. The other one was a vicious and destructive malevolence. In Part Two, the case studies describe circumstances that in some instances developed over time but came to a point of overwhelming crisis. Although these events did not necessarily come like a bolt of lightning out of a blue sky, nonetheless they were crushing and unexpected trials. One involved the disintegration of the minister's family. Another concerned disheartening dissension in the church congregation at the moment of its greatest opportunity. A third combined personal and church crises at the same time. Although the settings varied, each of the leaders faced challenges as never before.

The method for examining the case studies was initially to give a general narrative. We wrote the narratives from transcribed interviews that mostly reflected the perspectives of the primary leaders involved. Naturally, these perspectives may contain some biases. Therefore, upon transcribing the interviews, we diligently checked the facts against other sources as much as possible. All names and places in the accounts are as they were in the events with one exception. Because of the sensitivity of the material, the case study titled *First Baptist Church Oak Forest: When Trust Is Lost* uses pseudonyms for places and people. However, we did verify the accuracy of the details as in the other case studies.

The second part of each case study we have titled *Beyond the Story: Leadership Lessons*. In this section, we attempted to give a more global view and provide additional objectivity as well as some details of the aftermath. We noted the qualities of leadership that were the most critical, not only in the midst of the crisis but also for more normative leadership challenges. Every case study has a multitude of potential leadership insights and lessons, but we attempted to focus on those most relevant to the particular case study.

The last section of each case study features a set of questions for you to consider. We designed these to help you process the lessons highlighted by that case study. Our intent was to encourage you to evaluate your own understanding of leadership in some way through these questions.

In Part Three, we focused on help and hope for leaders. In the help chapter titled *Leadership Lifeboats*, we sought to point you to insights from various leadership authors and ultimately from a biblical perspective. While these principles are applicable to any setting, they find their ultimate purpose and effectiveness in ministry leadership. In the last chapter, titled *Aftermath*, our aim was to focus on the healing and grace that can be present in the most difficult of times. We utilized the experiences of two effective pastors to illustrate how God can provide hope and blessing in the new normal that follows a personal catastrophic crisis.

Speaking before the European Parliament concerning the global climate, Secretary of State Hillary Clinton admonished her audience to "never waste a good crisis."[10] Leaders have used this advice in various ways for centuries.[11] The phrase remains a relevant consideration. Crises inevitably come. Sometimes they come with astounding catastrophic intensity. In such moments, the overwhelming circumstances challenge leaders to the utmost. In recalling the events in our case studies, those interviewed were often surprised that they became emotional to the point of tears even though, for some, years had passed since the experience. It was apparent that the emotional scars of such crises do not heal very quickly and, in some instances, may never completely heal. In our effort to learn about the critical subject of leadership, we hope that the pain, stress, and suffering recorded in these case studies would not be in vain. The redemptive manifestation of God's grace was apparent in the midst of these catastrophic crises. We also believe that God has purposed to teach us lessons from them that ministry leaders cannot afford to ignore.

Notes

1. A. Malphurs, *Being Leaders: The Nature of Authentic Christian Leadership* (Grand Rapids: Baker, 2003), 63.

2. R. Banks and B. Ledbetter, *Reviewing Leadership: A Christian Evaluation of Current Approaches* (Grand Rapids: Baker, 2004), 21.

3. D. R. Conner, *Managing at the Speed of Change: How Resilient Managers Succeed and Prosper Where Others Fail* (New York: Villard Books, 1992), 3.

4. Banks and Ledbetter, *Reviewing Leadership*, 22.

5. B. N. Smith, R. V. Montagno, and T. N. Kuzmenko, "Transformational and Servant Leadership: Content and Contextual Comparisons," *Journal of Leadership and Organizational Studies* 22 (March 2004): 1.

6. B. George, 7 *Lessons for Leading in Crisis* (San Francisco: Jossey-Bass, 2009), 1.

7. H. B. Leonard, "Crisis," in *Encyclopedia of Leadership*, ed. G. R. Goethals, G. J. Sorenson, and J. McGregor Burns (Thousand Oaks, CA: Sage Publications), 1:290.

8. Ibid.

9. W. F. Arndt and F. W. Gingrich, *A Greek-English Lexicon of the New Testament and Other Early Christian Literature* (Chicago: University of Chicago Press, 1957), 420.

10. P. Harrison, "Never Waste a Good Crisis, Clinton Says on Climate," *Reuters Online*, March 7, 2009, http://in.reuters.com/article/environmentNews/idINTRE5251VN20090306 (accessed December 22, 2009).

11. Speakers and authors often attribute the quote "Never waste the opportunities offered by a good crisis" to Machiavelli's work *The Prince*, but the phrase does not appear in *The Prince*.

PART I

The Cataclysmic Event

HURRICANE DAMAGE MAP

NEW ORLEANS BAPTIST THEOLOGICAL SEMINARY

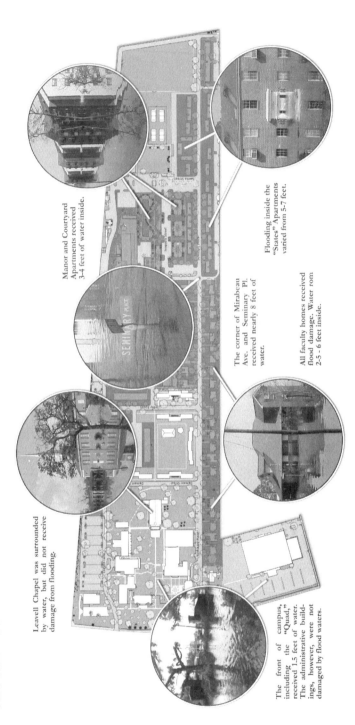

Leavell Chapel was surrounded by water, but did not receive damage from flooding.

Manor and Courtyard Apartments received 3-4 feet of water inside.

Flooding inside the "States" Apartments varied from 5-7 feet.

The corner of Mirabeau Ave. and Seminary Pl. received nearly 8 feet of water.

All faculty homes received flood damage. Water rom 2-5 - 6 feet inside.

The front of campus, including the "Quad," received 1.5 feet of water. The administrative buildings, however, were not damaged by flood waters.

Photos of the destruction of the flooding at various points on the campus of NOBTS. PHOTO BY GARY MYERS.

Chapter 1

The School of Providence and Prayer Faces Its Greatest Fear

"I will be with you when you pass through the waters."
Isaiah 43:2a

New Orleans Baptist Theological Seminary

Dr. Chuck Kelley spent four days on a roller coaster of emotions. Having evacuated from New Orleans, he was in a hotel room in Birmingham, Alabama, anxiously following the latest news reports on Hurricane Katrina. As president of New Orleans Baptist Theological Seminary (NOBTS), he and his administrative team were mindful of the vulnerability of New Orleans to hurricanes. They were well aware of the risk of "the big one" that had long been forecast.

Many had chronicled the potential catastrophic impact of a major hurricane on New Orleans. One widely noted warning had come in a series of articles in the major newspaper of the city, *The Times-Picayune*. Writers John McQuaid and Mark Schleifstein had noted that New Orleans was like a giant bowl surrounded by a levee system that protected it from the Gulf and the 630 square miles of Lake Pontchartrain. Hurricane Betsy, the last major hurricane to hit New Orleans (1965), left the city more vulnerable than ever before. The Gulf of Mexico was 20 miles closer because of the erosion of the marshland that previously served as a buffer of protection for New Orleans. In addition, a complex but dynamic process was causing the elevation of the city gradually to sink.[1] If the perfect storm hit, it would drive a massive surge from the Gulf of Mexico into Lake Pontchartrain, topping the levees and creating a new lake inside the city. With the average elevation of New Orleans being five feet below sea level, some experts believed that parts of the city could have as much as 30 feet of water. The potential damage would be horrific. Thousands could drown, and the city would likely be uninhabitable for months. New Orleans might never recover. Although the Army Corps of Engineers estimated that the odds of the levies being topped in such a storm were one in 300 in any given year, that prediction was little comfort on the day of one of the most catastrophic weather events in the history of the United States—the morning of August 29, 2005.[2]

For Kelley and the seminary leadership, the dramatic development of Katrina had begun several days earlier. On August 23, a tropical depression, the twelfth of the season, had formed over the southeastern Bahamas. On Thursday, August 25, shortly before landfall on the eastern coast of Florida, the storm became a minimal hurricane. As always with the development of an Atlantic tropical system, the seminary leadership had been monitoring Katrina. Initially, the storm had seemed to be no threat to New Orleans. As the storm went across Florida, it weakened to tropical storm status. Weather prognosticators expected it to emerge in the Gulf and move along the west coast of Florida. However, once it entered the Gulf of Mexico, extremely favorable climatic conditions caused a rare intensification of frightening proportions. By Saturday, the storm had reached major hurricane status. By Sunday, it broke the record for the strongest hurricane ever recorded in the Gulf of Mexico.

New Orleans Baptist Theological Seminary was known as the school of providence and prayer. This epithet originated from a vote of the annual Southern Baptist Convention meeting in 1917 to establish the school in an area where there were few Baptists or even evangelicals. The task was not an easy one, but the school established a firm presence for Southern Baptists in a city nicknamed "The Big Easy" because of its moral laxity. As a result, the New Orleans Baptist Theological Seminary family had a strong belief that only by providence and prayer had the school prospered in such a difficult environment. Following Katrina, that belief would be more critical to the survival of the seminary than at any time in its history.

Kelley and the administrative team had very little time to react. By the end of the campus workday on Friday, August 26, the projected storm track had shifted. It indicated a landfall along the Florida Panhandle or perhaps Mobile, Alabama, as the farthest westward target. With this prediction, campus residents who left town packed few belongings, planning to return after the weekend. However, on Saturday, Katrina's path changed again and New Orleans was now in the center of the projected landfall cone. The worst fears of the president and administrative team at New Orleans became a reality in the terrifying specter ominously consuming much of the Gulf of Mexico. In less than 48 hours, the storm had amassed the potential to obliterate the city and the seminary.

> *In less than 48 hours, the storm had amassed the potential to obliterate the city and the seminary.*

Those few hours had been frantic for Kelley. As president of the seminary, he had predetermined that he would stay and ride out any storm. He felt a deep sense of obligation to watch over the investment Southern Baptists had in New Orleans Baptist Theological Seminary. Besides, growing up on the coast of Texas, he had been through hurricanes before. His father had a funeral home business and always felt a duty to stay in order to serve the community. Chuck Kelley had the eye of one hurricane pass over him. No matter how fierce the storm, he could not conceive of leaving his beloved seminary. Like his father, he would stay out of a sense of responsibility to his vocation. His parents were another reason for staying. His 85-year-old father suffered from dementia, so his parents were residing in an assisted living apartment in New Orleans. Kelley's mother-in-law was living in the same facility, but she was out of town. The frantic pace of orchestrating an immediate and complete evacuation of the campus was stressful enough, but a serious concern for his parents also weighed on Kelley.

On Sunday, the administrative council had its final meeting before its members left the campus. Adding to the ominous mood of the meeting was the unprecedented mandatory evacuation order issued that morning by Ray Nagin, the mayor of New Orleans. However, Kelley was still insistent on remaining in New Orleans. As they were leaving, with very little time remaining to evacuate, the members of the council pleaded with him to leave as well. They pointed out that, if the storm were as severe as predicted, Kelley at the very least would be stranded in New Orleans and unable to communicate. This consequence would have been devastating for the seminary. Later he would express deep appreciation for his team telling him what he did not want to hear.

Time was running out for the president of NOBTS to evacuate. Although the New Orleans airport was about to close, a friend of the seminary offered to send a private plane to evacuate him. Before Kelley could make the decision, the friend called back to say the airport officials would not let the plane come in. The winds were already too high. Had he waited too late? What should he do about his parents? Traffic was gridlocked. With the window closing to leave before officials would shut down the interstate, there was no way to get to his parents in time. Even if he could, no place was available that could supply the care his father needed. Fortunately, Kelley's parents were in a strong multistory building on some of the highest ground in the city and less likely to flood. As it would be many times, God's provision was evident. At the last minute, a family friend stepped forward to provide care for his parents.

With barely time to throw a few items of clothing together, Chuck and his wife Rhonda evacuated by car to Birmingham. With the enormous traffic snarl, the normally six-hour trip stretched to 13 hours. As he drove, thoughts raced through his mind. Twenty-four campus security and maintenance personnel had remained to secure the campus. Would they be safe? The seminary was on some of the highest ground in the city. The front of the campus was slightly above sea level, and a number of sturdy buildings would provide a refuge. But there was still uncertainty. In modern history, New Orleans had never had a storm like Katrina. Leaving the seminary, his parents, and the remaining employees on the campus had been the most trying moment in Kelley's presidency of over nine years. It was the first of many difficult decisions he would make during the catastrophic crisis of Katrina.

On the evening of August 29, Chuck Kelley was still experiencing an emotional roller coaster. Four days earlier, the storm seemed to present no significant threat. The day before, Katrina threatened to wash away New Orleans from the face of the earth. At the last minute, there had been some hopeful news. Although still a major hurricane, the storm weakened before it came ashore. It also jogged to the east, striking along the border of Louisiana and Mississippi. News reports indicated that New Orleans had missed the worst of the storm's fury. Like many, as Katrina approached New Orleans, students at the North Georgia campus of NOBTS had been fervently praying. At a special chapel service on Monday morning, they rejoiced at the encouraging news. Now at approximately 4:30 p.m., the news was even more hopeful. Chris Friedmann, who was in charge of buildings and maintenance for the seminary, called Kelley to report that his crew of 24 was safe and that the damage to the seminary had been minimal. Friedmann was optimistic that once utility workers restored power it would be possible for classes to meet within a few days. Chuck Kelley hung up the phone with an enormous sense of relief and thanksgiving to God. He and his wife went out to dinner that evening with the feeling that indeed everything would be all right. They went to bed with no reason to think differently, but that feeling would be short-lived.

> *. . . when he and his crew saw live shrimp and fish in the water, their worst fears became a reality.*

Friedmann and his crew had been staying in a secure location at the front of the seminary campus. That night some of them went back to their homes and apartments. As he approached his house, Friedmann had noticed that the water had risen to halfway up his front yard. Exhausted, he tried to sleep, but the air was hot, stuffy, and humid. About midnight, Chris got up and looked out from the front of the house to see that the water had risen ominously to the point where it would soon be in his house. The seriousness of the situation was becoming more evident. Later, when he and his crew saw live shrimp and fish in the water, their worst fears became a reality.[3] The levees along the canals that normally drain water into Lake Pontchartrain were failing. Although New Orleans escaped the brunt of Katrina, the massive storm surge that exceeded 20 feet had pushed more water into the lake than the levees could hold. The seminary and the city were in serious trouble.

On Tuesday, the dire news reports began to come in. The gaps in the levees had grown, and massive amounts of water were inundating the city. Communication with the seminary campus ceased, and for three days Kelley and his administrative team would have no way of knowing the fate of the crew or the extent of the damage to the seminary. First and foremost, the president was concerned with the safety of the crew. In addition to fearing danger from the flooding, Kelley received a report that police and the National Guard had exchanged gunfire with looters and anarchists close to the campus. Kelley later would learn that the campus faced a serious threat from the riotous behavior of some in the community. Looters were performing random acts of destruction and violence. What might they do to the crew? Even if the crew managed to remain safe, what might the looters do to the most essential building on campus, the library? With one of the largest theological collections in the nation, the seminary could ill afford to lose its library. If the seminary were ever to be up and running again, the library resources would be of critical importance in maintaining accreditation.

Communication is essential for leadership in the midst of a crisis. Chuck Kelley was woefully short on information from the campus, but he found another communication was undisturbed: his communication with God. At that moment of such incredible stress and uncertainty, God brought to his mind Psalm 46. Kelley recalled that he and Rhonda read the passage, and "[we] just got down on our knees and I just committed the situation to God, and He filled our soul with peace." From that moment on, if he ever felt overwhelmed, "it never lasted very long [because] God just kept that peace there." Further undergirding Kelley was an assurance of his calling. He noted that it was this certainty of calling that enabled him to have the confidence to make decisions. His confidence came from "knowing that God has been getting me ready all of my life for this moment in space and time." With that conviction, Kelley moved forward with a decisiveness that would prove to be crucial in the hectic and chaotic first few days.

The first important decision Kelley had to make in the aftermath of the storm was how to get the administrative team together as quickly as possible. Kelley found himself torn between a pastoral role and an administrative role. He felt deeply for the team members' losses and knew they all had families experiencing the trauma of the catastrophe. Yet he was responsible for the seminary, and he discerned that time was critical. Students were scattered to 29 states and faculty to nine states. Soon they could be making irrevocable decisions to plant their lives in places other than New Orleans. The stakes were enormous. If too many students or faculty relocated, the seminary would have difficulty surviving even if the city did. Some members of the administrative team requested that they not be required to be in Atlanta until after Labor Day. The extra time would allow them to deal with critical family needs. Reluctantly, Kelley declined their requests. He felt it was imperative that the seminary leadership immediately signal that the administrative team was functioning and moving forward. He instructed these leaders that no matter what it took to get there, they were to be in Atlanta in three days.

With nearly 400 students, the North Georgia Center of NOBTS was one of the largest theological extension centers in the nation. Kelley called it "the crown jewel" of the NOBTS extension center system. Located in Decatur, Georgia, the center occupied a large church building complex, which Columbia Drive Baptist Church had donated to NOBTS. The gift of the facility some 10 years earlier proved to be a godsend, as it would become the temporary home of the operations of NOBTS.

In addition to meeting with his administrative team, one of Kelley's initial actions was to have a brainstorming session with the displaced seminary family that first began to trickle in and then pour in to the Atlanta campus. Four days after the storm hit, Kelley stood before the bedraggled group and asked them to identify the challenges ahead. He wrote them on a board, categorized them, and quickly appointed task forces to handle the issues. Some of the seminary leadership questioned the wisdom of having such an open session. Would false expectations be raised? However, no issues were presented that had not already been in the minds of the administrative team. Nonetheless, this action served two purposes: it brought a focus on moving forward, and it provided a mechanism for the seminary staff and faculty to feel that they could give input.

Various teams swung into action. Housing for students and faculty was critical. The Georgia Baptist Convention and numerous churches stepped forward to meet the need. Information technology personnel worked tirelessly to get the seminary back online from the new location in Atlanta. It would be weeks before faculty could have access to material from their offices and staff could retrieve computer data for the most basic seminary functions. Yet creative improvisation made things work in new ways. Incredibly, in the midst of it all, the seminary never missed a payroll.

With teams working to meet the needs of the seminary family, a critical question needed an immediate answer. Would the seminary continue to teach, or would it do as every other educational system in New Orleans had done and simply shut down for at least the fall semester? At this point, Kelley made two decisions that would prove to play a huge part in the survival of the seminary: NOBTS would continue teaching for the fall semester, and there would be a December graduation. Intuitively, Kelley was relying on the hope that most of the students would want to continue their fall classes if possible. Kelley did not have specific information on student feelings at the time of the decision, but his instinct proved to be correct. A massive effort to contact the students later revealed that 85 percent of them desired to continue.

The decisions to continue full teaching and to have a December graduation became a certainty upon which the seminary could rally their efforts. Teaching courses "gave people a routine to have when they were living in an unfamiliar place," Kelley said. With the seminary family scattered, "cohesion was really tough." Kelley further observed, "If you're going to pull people out of the catastrophe, you have to have a vision above the catastrophe that they can see."

As difficult as it would be to carry out these plans, the seminary was in a unique position to succeed. One favorable aspect was the large off-campus program of the seminary. The nearly 400 students in Atlanta were just a small part of the over 1,700 students in the seminary's 16 centers in Florida, Alabama, Georgia, Mississippi, and Louisiana. These centers represented approximately 47 percent of the seminary's total enrollment. Many of the students had gone to areas where they could take courses at one of the centers. However, these centers represented only five states, and students were in 29. How would the professors teach them? The answer was the internet.

Fortunately, NOBTS had been integrating technology into the classroom. The BlackBoard system was capable of allowing students to take their classes fully online. Significant barriers were present. Every faculty member would need a laptop along with crash training programs for them to learn internet teaching techniques. The faculty response to this task was nothing short of phenomenal. If the faculty had responded that they were not able to teach a full semester schedule, Kelley freely admitted that there would have been little that he could have done otherwise. He called their efforts "the stuff of legends" and "the most heroic performance by a faculty in the history of the world."

Kelley well understood that the relocation of the operations of the seminary to Atlanta brought hardships. Because the time for evacuation had been short, the faculty who fled New Orleans left with few possessions. Many evacuated to family who could house them, and it would be months if not a full year before they could return to their homes in New Orleans. Since they would be teaching through the internet, it was natural for them to want to remain near the family support to which they had fled. For those without administrative responsibilities, this arrangement would work well. However, in the NOBTS structure, a large percentage of the faculty had significant administrative duties. Thus, Kelley required most of them to be present at the Atlanta site. The sacrifices for many of them to go to Atlanta would be great. Some faculty had children with special needs. Others had members of their immediate family in more than one state. The hardship circumstances of this group were legitimate and in many cases overwhelming. Not surprisingly, Kelley's insistence that they work at the Atlanta location resulted in serious discontent among some faculty members. A significant percentage of staff members required to be in Atlanta faced similar adversity and accompanying feelings. Later, Kelley often expressed his deepest appreciation for the ones who made these very difficult sacrifices.

In an early attempt to boost faculty morale and establish a forward direction, Kelley set a meeting of the NOBTS campus family and their spouses to occur 10 days after the hurricane. The meeting would be held at Southwestern Baptist Theological Seminary (SWBTS) in Forth Worth, Texas. Although at the time Kelley was not sure how the seminary could pay for it, he told the faculty to get there any way they could and NOBTS would reimburse them. In the meantime, Kelley and his vice president for business affairs had been scrambling for a way to give the faculty some immediate support. It came in the form of substantial help from some state conventions as well as other sources. At the meeting at SWBTS, the faculty members each received a check for $1,000 and some WalMart gift cards. One Sunday school class from the First Baptist Church of Euless, Texas, filled a room with clothing of all sizes for faculty families. Beyond providing for immediate needs, this reminded the seminary family they would not walk through the crisis alone.

The gathering at SWBTS was also a time of grieving. A particularly trying experience was seeing the slides of campus destruction. All but the very front of the campus had water in the buildings. The lowest point in the back of the campus had eight feet of water. Fortunately, the library and all the academic buildings, including the chapel, escaped encroachment from floodwaters. Yet in many cases, even these buildings had significant water damage from torrential rain that poured through damaged windows or roofs.

Going through the photos of the damaged residences of students and faculty was a particularly arduous leadership episode for Kelley. The president's home occupied the highest ground on the campus and was not flooded, but the area where the faculty resided was. Kelley found himself where many leaders are in a catastrophic crisis, deeply affected by the crisis but not always in an equivalent way as their constituents. He described

> *Kelley found himself where many leaders are in a catastrophic crisis, deeply affected by the crisis but not always in an equivalent way as their constituents.*

the entire experience of going through these slides as "the most emotionally difficult thing" to that point. But another tough decision was on the horizon for Kelley and his leadership team.

Other educational institutions in New Orleans had not only let go staff but also had massive faculty layoffs. Some were urging Kelley to do the same. However, Kelley knew he must do everything possible to keep the faculty whom he considered "the heart and soul" of the seminary. Since NOBTS would continue teaching classes, Kelley decided there would be no faculty layoffs. At this point, Kelley was dependent on God's provision, which had been his assurance from the beginning. One example of such provision was that no institution in the city received insurance funds quicker than NOBTS. Numerous gifts also came in with seemingly divine timing. Miraculously and sometimes just barely, the seminary was able to keep its complete resident faculty on payroll and meet its other obligations. The effort to help faculty and staff would be a constant emphasis of NOBTS throughout the Katrina experience. When the cost of returning to the campus seemed almost out of reach, it would have been tempting to limit aid to those moving back. Yet the commitment to assist employees in every way possible remained steadfast. No other institution in New Orleans did proportionately what NOBTS and Southern Baptists did for faculty, staff, and students. The final tally of this aid would be well over a million dollars.

One of the toughest leadership challenges was to balance the needs of the victims of the campus flooding with the need to get the seminary campus back to functioning as soon as possible. Decisively, in the first few days of the crisis, Kelley arranged for a Christian contractor who had done work for the seminary for a number of years to begin planning for rebuilding the campus. A more formal and deliberative bid process would have lessened the potential for criticism, but Kelley recognized that there simply was not enough time to follow the normal procedure. In the face of a catastrophic crisis, he would have to do the unconventional. Fortunately for the seminary, the contractor began immediately booking materials and enlisting workers. At a later time, materials and workers would be almost impossible to secure. The seminary began to rebuild before other institutions could even consider doing so. The undertaking was so massive that every day was critical to having the campus ready for the new school year in the fall of 2006. An essential condition of the agreement for the contractor to attempt such an undertaking was that the campus would be clear of residents for the entire reconstruction period. Only for five days, October 5–9, could he allow former residents back to sift through belongings. This process would prove to be extremely emotionally charged and rife with potential for conflict.

The brevity of the period for retrieval of items was difficult for some to accept. Prior to this time, numerous individuals had wanted access to the campus—and with good reasons. Three weeks of standing water had made material on lower floors virtually useless. Campus residents who had items on upper floors and in attics hoped to find them still usable. However, the growth of mold was astounding, quickly ruining even items untouched by the water. Priceless photographs, mementos, and valuable antiques would not last long under such conditions. Time was of the essence.

For Chuck Kelley, having to tell people they could retrieve their belongings only during the designated five-day period was one of the toughest decisions of the crisis. First, he was concerned for people's health and safety. With debris everywhere, the campus was a dangerous place. Many buildings were unsafe to enter because of continued crumbling from the destruction of the flood and the efforts of the construction crews. Second, the contractor could not maintain the construction schedule for getting the campus ready for the next full school year if access was not controlled. Third, it would have been unfair for Kelley to allow some residents to enter the campus and not others, regardless of extenuating circumstances.

Although they may not have agreed with the restrictions, the overwhelming majority of the seminary family responded with grace. Unfortunately, some did not. No matter what rationale the seminary leadership gave, to them the restrictions seemed harsh and uncaring. In the stress of great loss and grief, they lost emotional control. The security staff guarding the gate faced some who were belligerent. In those instances, Kelley had instructed the security personnel to give upset individuals his cell phone number. He fielded innumerable calls. Those who had crossed the line with their language and behavior, he had to chastise. He reminded them that they had a call to the gospel ministry and that certain actions and attitudes were inappropriate regardless of the stress. It was not a happy task.

Kelley realized that as president, his role in helping the faculty, staff, and students cope with their grief and loss would be vital. During the time the seminary family was back on the campus, the heat was oppressive. Kelley constantly distributed bottled water and listened to their heart-aches and grief. Conscious of the need to connect with people, he was the only one on campus not wearing a mask and other protective gear. This action was risky, as toxins from the horrific growth of mold and chemical residues from putrid floodwaters contaminated the campus. But Kelley felt it was essential that the seminary family be able to see his face, which would communicate his genuine concern and empathy. As the former residents of the campus sorted through the muck of the aftermath, very little that remained was salvageable. The pastoral sup-port of the president and volunteers who came to help was immensely important.

By the end of the fall semester, the seminary had achieved significant steps toward recovery. The graduation ceremony occurred on Decem-ber 17, 2005, at the Church of Brook Hills in Birmingham, Alabama. With 137 graduates and a large attendance, the event was the capstone of finishing the semester despite the obstacles. Gradually, workers were making progress in rebuilding the campus. In early January 2006, Kelley returned to his home despite the lack of reliable phone service or power. A few restored apartments became available for key administrators. The seminary held classes for commuter students on a block schedule on a limited basis. It was a small start, but it gave enormous hope. By the beginning of the fall 2006 semester, the seminary had completed a sub-stantial portion of the rebuilding of the campus. Students who had been through the storm returned in large numbers, and despite the risks, new students were undaunted in their call to come to NOBTS. The 2006–7 academic year would yield a total enrollment equal to 90 percent of the record enrollment of the year prior to the catastrophic crisis of Katrina. For months after the reopening of the campus, on the fence at the front of the campus hung a banner with the words: "When we passed through the waters, God was with us." It was a reflection of the promise found in Isa 43:2. The NOBTS family had experienced the fulfillment of this promise.

Beyond the Story: Leadership Lessons

Visionary Leadership

Catastrophic crises do not come with a leadership manual. Instead, the leadership must come from principles already imbedded in the leader's style as well as a willingness to take risks based on best judgment. For President Chuck Kelley, these characteristics would play out in his leadership role in the midst of the Katrina crisis in several ways. Perhaps the most prominent aspect of his leadership style the one that would make the greatest impact, was his visionary leadership.

During Kelley's tenure as president of NOBTS, the seminary had seen enormous growth, essentially doubling in total headcount in a little less than 10 years. He had been the chief instigator of this growth by holding forth a vision of some new approaches that proved successful in drawing students to what some considered a disadvantaged location for a seminary. Kelley dealt with this attitude head on. He included all elements of NOBTS in an examination of the effect of the seminary's location that would culminate in a resounding, unanimous vote by the trustees to remain in New Orleans. Kelley utilized the NOBTS theme of being the school of providence and prayer to turn the perceived negative into a positive. NOBTS affirmed even more strongly that the providence of God had placed the school in the perfect strategic place for ministry. Kelley asserted that the world was becoming increasingly urban and diverse, more like New Orleans than a homogeneous suburb or a small Southern community. What environment would be better than New Orleans for preparing students for twenty-first-century ministry? The vision casting worked. Students came in record numbers.

The conviction concerning this vision for being in New Orleans proved crucial for the survival of the seminary. In the early days of the Katrina crisis, the trustees met and again unanimously affirmed that New Orleans would continue to be the home of the seminary. Many outside the seminary family as well as some inside the NOBTS world would question that decision. However, the trustees' verdict settled the issue. Out of this affirmation flowed other critical decisions. The shared vision provided the administrative team with an ability to prioritize in the midst of a sea of demands.

Throughout the crisis, Chuck Kelley would be the highly visible, visionary leader, the one who believed against all odds that God had destined the recovery of the seminary. During the early weeks of recovery, the seminary had been a beacon of hope on the eastern side of the city. Because of the contractor's extreme efforts, NOBTS was one of the first areas on the east side to receive power. At night, when travelers entered New Orleans from the east via Interstate 10 and came to the pinnacle of the High Rise bridge over the Industrial Canal, they emerged from a vast stretch of darkness to see a shining ray of hope: the lights from the chapel steeple on the NOBTS campus. Kelley reminded the seminary family that this was a dramatic visual reminder that God had placed them in the city to be a light in the midst of spiritual darkness. He believed the strategic importance of New Orleans would ensure its rebuilding. Kelley was convinced that returning to New Orleans would afford an unprecedented ministry opportunity for NOBTS. In the aftermath, his vision proved true as thousands of Baptists worked in disaster relief efforts immediately following the storm, and even years after, through the Mission Lab program of the seminary. New Orleans was more open to the gospel than it had ever been before.

> *Throughout the crisis, Chuck Kelley would be the highly visible, visionary leader, the one who believed against all odds that God had destined the recovery of the seminary.*

Creative Leadership

Another aspect of Kelley's leadership style that served well was his willingness to do the unconventional. Prior to taking the presidency, as both a student and a professor for many years, he had called his ministry "Innovative Evangelism." Chuck Kelley had a knack for doing things creatively and successfully, and he employed this talent early in his critical decision-making process. Kelley noted that whatever "book that is there for disasters in terms of business operations says that the very first thing you do is reduce all of your expenses to the point that you know you can cover your expenses and you can build back later as you know more of your situation." By not laying off faculty, Kelley threw out the book. In hindsight, this decision to go against conventional wisdom kept the seminary from splintering to a degree that full recovery might have been impossible. It was one of several times that Kelley's willingness to do the counterintuitive would yield positive results.

Flexible Leadership

According to a number of leadership authors and experts, the ability to adapt one's leadership style is critical, especially in crises. Dexterity in alternating between the roles of a strong commanding leader and affiliate leader is one manifestation of this skill.[4] In a crisis, leaders often must make quick decisions and set forth high expectations, but also know when to be empathetic. Kelley observed that "you have to know when to push people, but you also have to know when to pat people on the back and say, 'you know, you are doing a great job,' and, 'you know, let's ease up a little bit.'" Like all leaders, in the midst of the complexity of a crisis Kelley was subject to having an imperfect balance between the two. Yet his ability to use both styles was evident. He utilized the former in the accomplishment of the return to the main campus in seemingly miraculous time. He demonstrated the latter by the fact that over 80 percent of the trustee-elected faculty were in place at the start of the 2005–6 academic year.

The Challenge of the New Normal

When a catastrophic crisis occurs, the leader must deal with the aftermath. A crisis brings a new normal. In the case of NOBTS, the challenge was significant. The seminary could claim "a miracle on the Mississippi" concerning the reconstruction of the facilities and the enrollment recovery, but these achievements did not mean life was the same. One aspect was what Kelley called the "adrenalin factor." As Kelley noted, during the Katrina year the faculty and staff of the seminary performed with maximum effort. Students likewise faced enormous challenges and overcame them. Despite the natural uplift in returning to the campus, an inevitable fatigue followed living on the adrenalin. Exhaustion and post-traumatic stress—which many of the seminary family experienced—made motivation to move forward a tremendous challenge.

In a very specific way, Kelley felt that the fatigue and trauma experienced by the faculty led to a failure to make a quick transition to a permanent inclusion of substantial course offerings via the internet. Kelley envisioned a delivery system in which geography would not be a limitation in receiving theological education. Since the faculty had taught courses through the internet, Kelley thought that the transition to a more internet-based delivery system would be easy. However, as in most crises, the tendency is to want to return to the familiar, not the innovative. Kelley found that "after the crisis was over it resulted in a much greater resistance to change than we had before the storm." In addition, communication on the issue was a problem. Kelley admitted that he had underestimated the need for communication for the seminary to move forward with an expanded emphasis on the internet. The communication on his part would need to be more specific and overt. Overall, the leadership team needed a

> *Kelley admitted, "It was one of the things that I did not handle very well."*

more effective feedback loop to hear from the faculty about how to work out the barriers to accomplishing the president's vision. For a leader with a strong vision of future opportunities at the seminary, the inability to move forward quickly with a new delivery system paradigm was difficult to accept. Kelley admitted, "It was one of the things that I did not handle very well."

Since communication was a huge factor during both the crisis and post-crisis periods, it was important to be as effective as possible. In the challenge of communicating, Kelley felt the pull of conflicting advice from seminary leadership. Some advised him not to give status reports unless he had new information. Frequent messages with no progress to relate might produce frustration. Others urged him to issue regular updates, even if no new information were available, to provide a morale boost that just hearing from the leader of the seminary would bring. During the crisis, Kelley leaned more toward the former, even though he was well aware that some might interpret this approach as remoteness. The lack of frequent updates resulted in confusion on some issues among the seminary family. In retrospect, Kelley determined that redundancy of communication at all levels would have been helpful.

A new awareness of vulnerability was an indelible mark left by the crisis. Reflecting on preparation for the possibility of a future "big one," Kelley asserted, "Hurricane season will come again. . . . And we are going to be ready." A comprehensive plan for coping with a worst-case scenario was developed. Specific aspects included having all faculty members ready with a plan for putting their classes online. All departments have backups of their computer data ready to take with them. Every hurricane season, the seminary rents a large truck for transporting the servers to the Atlanta site, where the Information Technology department could relocate and be operational within 24 hours. In addition, true to the lesson he learned about communication, during the next evacuation in 2008 for Hurricane Gustav, Kelley issued several status reports each day. Even though he received criticism for giving updates without any significant new information, he decided that staying in touch was essential.

One reality of the new normal was that, for some, a year away from New Orleans meant a change of life that no longer included the seminary. A significant number of longtime staff did not return. With nearly 20 percent of the faculty leaving before the start of the 2006–7 year and normal attrition each year afterward, gradually an increasing percentage of the faculty had not experienced Katrina. Although he had frequently given homage to the heroic efforts of the Katrina faculty, Kelley felt that the seminary needed to move on. In the August 2008 faculty retreat, he addressed the subject in a dramatic fashion. He turned to one side and gave a final soliloquy and physical salute of praise to the efforts of the Katrina faculty. He then turned back to face the current faculty and reminded them that the faculty that was present during Katrina no longer existed. It was time for the current faculty to take up the new challenges they faced. The strategy was risky with Katrina wounds still fresh for a number of faculty members, but one he felt was necessary in order for the faculty to embrace the new future.

Kelley and the NOBTS seminary family hope that another day like August 29, 2005 will never come. However, if it does come, the residents of the New Orleans campus are there because they believe they are answering a calling. No matter what happens, they are willing to face the circumstances. They believe that a place of challenges and risks is the perfect setting for training the next generation of ministers who must face their own uncertainties. The school of providence and prayer and its seminary family cannot claim perfect safety, but they can claim the certainty of the promises of Psalm 46.

Questions for Further Thought

1. In the midst of a crisis, should a leader give regular updates if there is no new information?
2. In a catastrophic crisis, how can a leader who has not experienced direct personal loss identify with those who have?
3. Every leader faces risks in the midst of a crisis. What were the risks of Kelley's early decisive actions? What would have been the risks of a more deliberate approach?
4. In a crisis, is it more difficult for the leader to challenge constituents to exceptionally high performance or to meet the pastoral needs of the traumatized? What are some possible pitfalls in attempting to strike a balance?
5. Why do leaders sometimes have to "throw out the book" in a crisis? What are the risks?
6. Why is it not possible to go back to the old normal after a crisis? What emotional factors could tempt the leader to try to return to the old normal?
7. How can a crisis impact the willingness of an organization to change to meet the new challenges and opportunities it inevitably will face?

Notes

1. J. McQuaid and M. Schleifstein, "Washing Away," *The Times-Picayune*, June 23, 2002, J2.

2. McQuaid and Schleifstein, "The Big One," *The Times-Picayune*, June 24, 2002, A1, A7.

3. G. Myers, "As Floodwater Rose at Seminary, Crew Faced Mounting Crisis," *Baptist Press*, September 15, 2005.

4. D. Goleman, R. Boyatzis, and A. McKee, *Primal Leadership: Realizing the Power of Emotional Intelligence* (Boston: Harvard Business School Press, 2002), 53.

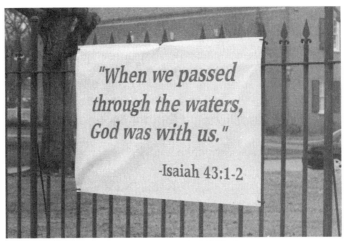

Post-Katrina banner on front entrance of NOBTS Campus. PHOTO BY GARY MYERS.

Flooding on the NOBTS campus. PHOTO BY GARY MYERS.

Chapter 2

An Opportunity in a Whirlwind

"Then the Lord answered Job from the whirlwind." Job 38:1a

Bethel Baptist Church

Wednesday nights at Bethel Baptist Church in Moody, Alabama, tradition-
ally had drawn large numbers of people to the various scheduled activities. On a fateful Wednesday night before Easter in April 1998, everything
was in high gear. With members practicing for a major music presentation just days away, the church was more crowded than normal. Weather
forecasts earlier in the day had mentioned the possibility of strong
storms that evening, but such spring weather was typical for Alabama.
People had come to expect that these systems would produce little more
than a brief thunderstorm with perhaps an accompanying downpour
and higher-than-normal winds. Yes, an infamous F4 tornado had struck
during a Palm Sunday service four years earlier at the Goshen United
Methodist Church in Piedmont, Alabama, a small town approximately 50
miles northeast of Moody. Twenty people perished in that tornado. The
Birmingham media's extensive coverage of the tragedy touched many

Destruction of the old worship center by the tornado. PHOTO BY JULIE ECHOLS.

Tornado destruction of the partly built new worship center (right) and other buildings. PHOTO BY JULIE ECHOLS.

Alabamians deeply. However, that event seemed long ago, and what were the odds of another church in that part of the state being struck? The staff could not cancel services for every remote threat of severe weather, especially the Wednesday before Easter.

Bethel Baptist Church in many ways typified a church that was transitioning from a rural to a suburban ministry. The community had grown rapidly, and with the promised construction of a large auto plant nearby, the potential for continued growth seemed extremely promising. In the previous 20 years, church attendance had swelled from a little more than 100 to over 500. The facilities of the church were not adequate for the current attendance, let alone the potential for an even greater increase. Accordingly, the membership initiated an ambitious building program. After the completion of the children's building, a debate arose as to what the next building would be: a new worship center or a family life center. The pastor and the leadership boldly decided to do both.

The campaign to raise the funds for the buildings had been a spectacular success, and plans moved forward. Yet obstacles still existed. One challenge was the layout of the existing buildings. Although the congregation had developed a careful long-range plan to utilize the 15-acre site, the positioning of structures that existed prior to the new children's building was a problem.

> *. . . maybe God would do the church a favor and remove the old buildings at a time when they would be unoccupied and the church could collect the insurance.*

Two buildings in particular prevented the ideal in land use and floor space and the optimum for functionality and traffic flow. To work around the location of these older buildings seemed more challenging than the proverbial Gordian knot. In a moment of dark humor, the previous pastor privately remarked to some of the staff that maybe God would do the church a favor and remove the old buildings at a time when they would be unoccupied and the church could collect the insurance. Little could that pastor have imagined that such an event would occur.

Bethel Baptist Church would meet as usual on that Wednesday evening before Easter. By 8:00 p.m., all the regular activities had concluded. However, approximately 100 people were still practicing for the Easter musical. As the evening progressed, the approaching weather system looked more ominous. A member who lived near the church campus had been watching the updated information, and he passed the latest report on to the associate pastor, Randy Gunter. As the storm moved eastward from the adjacent county, officials observed severe tornado activity. At its current speed, the storm would be in Moody in less than an hour.

Upon hearing of the severity of the approaching storm, Randy went immediately to the worship minister, Barry Daniel. Barry and Randy concluded that finding safe shelter at the church for the large number of people who were there would be chaotic and dangerous. Most of the buildings of the church were not strong enough to withstand tornado-force winds. While the new family life center was substantially complete, it was not ready for occupancy. The new worship center was only about one-third complete. With construction material everywhere, even substantial straight-line winds might make deadly missiles of the debris. How much more deadly would a tornado be? It was a frightening thought. With these factors in mind, it was apparent that people would be less at risk in their own homes. Judging by the position of the storm, the congregation would have just enough time to evacuate to their homes safely if they acted quickly.

With the Easter musical imminent, Pastor Chris Burns knew that shortening the rehearsal would not be easy for Barry. "I would rather go ahead and send the people home while our weather is not bad and then it get bad here and then have to send them home. How do you feel about that?" Barry asked Chris. "Man, absolutely. You're in charge of the music program here. Whatever you're comfortable with, because you know what you've got to do Sunday. I don't. So let the folks go home," Chris responded. It was only in the aftermath that Chris, Barry, and Randy would find out how divinely guided their decision had been.

At approximately 8:20 p.m., Chris and the staff quickly informed everyone of the potential threat and urged them to seek shelter immediately in the safest possible location in either their own home or that of a friend, family member, or neighbor. People wasted little time leaving.

Within 15 minutes, the evacuation was completed and the buildings locked. The pastor and the custodian were the last to leave; they had gone through the buildings to make sure everyone was out before locking up. The custodian asked whether he could bring his family to the church since he lived in a double-wide trailer. The pastor agreed that he should do whatever he felt was safest for his family. At approximately 8:35 p.m., the pastor and the custodian left. The storm struck at 8:56 p.m.

A few minutes after Randy got home, the weather turned ominous. Seeking shelter in a closet in the middle of their house, Randy and his wife and two small children could not help but be frightened by the sound of the violent wind. They were thankful that it lasted only minutes and that their house and those in their immediate area escaped any serious damage. The relief was short-lived, since a few minutes after the wind passed, Randy received a report from the pastor that a tornado had struck the church facilities.

Chris also had experienced the strong winds. Like Randy, he was grateful that neither he nor his neighbors had suffered any significant damage. Suddenly a call came from a friend who lived near the church. He told Chris that the church had been hit, "and it looks pretty bad." Chris was stunned and thought his friend was kidding. How could the tornado have hit the church so hard when his home sustained no serious damage and was only two miles away? However, the tone of the friend's voice was convincing. The church had received a direct hit. Later, Chris learned that the cause of the damage was a high-intensity F2 tornado that came down directly on the church and then bounced away as suddenly as it had come. Believing that the worst of the storm was past and that his family was safe, Chris drove toward the church.

> *Chris was unprepared for what he saw. The powerful winds had twisted the erected steel of the new worship center like spaghetti.*

Less than a half mile from the church, the police had already closed the road. Because he was the pastor, the officers immediately let him through.

Chris was unprepared for what he saw. The powerful winds had twisted the erected steel of the new worship center like spaghetti. With the exception of the children's wing, the tornado had made rubble of all the buildings. The immediate concern for Chris was the custodian and his family. Had he brought his family to the church for shelter? A careful search revealed no one in the buildings. Then a comforting call came from one of the members, who said that at the last moment the custodian had decided to seek safety in a neighbor's house, which had a basement. Remarkably, the tornado had made a quick touchdown at the church and had left most of the area surrounding the church with only minor damage.

The only people in danger in the vicinity of the church were storm chasers. Their van with a front tag that said "cyclone chaser" was upside down. The wind had blown it 50 yards across the church parking lot. They were amazingly unharmed and quickly left the scene. With news of the safety of the custodian and the storm chasers, and with the confirmation that no one was in the buildings when the tornado struck, Chris felt a sense of relief. "No one is hurt. That is what matters. Everything else can be repaired," Chris thought. He knew the church had good insurance coverage. The two buildings under construction were the responsibility of the contractor, a church member who also had insurance coverage. Chris felt confident that the church eventually would have all the facilities replaced. But how would it cope with the immediate logistics? The task seemed overwhelming.

Like Chris, Randy was relieved to learn that no one was hurt. However, he experienced an overwhelming sense of grief. Bethel was Randy's home church. For him, the buildings held many cherished memories. In addition, as the administrator, Randy was the staff member responsible for overseeing the construction. One building program was challenging enough. Two at one time had been extremely taxing. Nonetheless, the anticipation of a dream had made the effort seem worthwhile. Now that dream had become crumpled buildings and twisted steel. For a few moments, he could not hold back the tears. However, he quickly regained control of his emotions. There was little time for grieving. In the morning, he would face the first steps in the task of rebuilding with the pastor and other leaders. Randy later reflected that the recovery effort so consumed him that he never had a chance to go through a grieving process. Even when recalling the event years later, sometimes he could feel the emotion welling up. Through this experience, Randy realized it would take time for the church to work through the loss. No one instance could provide a complete catharsis from years of emotional attachment to the destroyed facilities.

Randy felt the heavy pressure of his responsibilities. The congregation greatly respected his administrative skills. As a result, the pastor, staff team, and other church leaders had let him take the bulk of the decision making for everything about the building program. Now he would be in charge of the rebuild. In retrospect, he considered this singular delegation of duties a mistake. "I realized that even after the fact . . . I was carrying way too much of the building, way too much of the decisions, way too much of the victory and now I realized that was why I was carrying the weight of the destruction. . . . If I had included more people in the process, then they could have helped me carry some of the weight of the destruction as well," Randy later confessed.

The day after the tornado brought a resolve from the staff and church leaders to move forward. The many details of preparing for Easter Sunday seemed overwhelming. However, the leadership matrix at Bethel was a healthy model to have in a crisis. Pastor Chris Burns believed in allowing people to exercise their spiritual gifts without a sense of rivalry. Randy remarked, "Chris really afforded me more leadership than what most pastors would." For his part, Chris would acknowledge, "God put somebody really special beside me with Randy Gunter." Chris had given Randy the responsibility of managing the building program, and now he would trust him with the details of the reconstruction. The pastor would be informed and attend key meetings, but the details were left to Randy. As a result, Chris was free to perform some important functions for which he was well suited. He would be able to invest in ministering to the people and handling all the public-relations issues. This arrangement worked well since Randy admitted that he was much less comfortable than Chris in these matters. Chris's philosophy of empowering leaders and releasing them to their tasks proved invaluable, not only with Randy but also with other church leaders who ministered during the crisis.

One of the things that became apparent was that the crisis would allow a bypassing of the traditional methods of doing things. The church generally understood that there would not be time to have a committee meeting for every decision. Randy quickly put together what was referred to as the "immediate response team." It consisted of people who knew how to get things done—business people, multitaskers, and members who had extensive contacts in the community.

A key strategy early on was to focus on the most urgent priorities. The immediate response team could not waste time speculating about what the rebuilt church would look like. The time for that would come later. Yes, insurance people and the contractor needed some attention, but it was Thursday and Sunday was coming. What would Bethel Baptist Church do for Easter? The Easter activities would be critical. If Sunday went well, it would be a powerful witness to the community that God would enable the church to overcome the crisis. Interestingly, in addition to the denomination and other churches, it would be through the surrounding communities of Moody and Odenville that some of the most important support would come.

One of the most pressing concerns was the planned Easter musical and drama. In the aftermath of the tornado, the extensive preparation now seemed useless. Where could the church possibly find a place that would be suitable to put on such a large production? What would they do about sound equipment and instruments? The answer came quickly to Chris with a call from the pastor at First Baptist of Moody asking whether Bethel Baptist had been planning to do an Easter musical. Chris responded with a melancholy "Yeah." "When do you want to present it?" the Moody pastor asked. Chris answered in amazement, "What do you mean?" "Our church is open. . . . We are ready for it," the pastor offered. Chris was encouraged. Being able to perform the Easter musical would be a huge morale booster for the church.

The next critical decision was what to do about Sunday morning. Easter morning was the biggest attendance of the year. With the tornado certain to bring out the curious, Sunday promised to be the largest crowd in Bethel's history. But where would they meet? Chris had developed some relationships that would reap dividends. He knew the superintendent of the school system and the principal of Moody High School quite well. They granted permission for the church to use the gym at a minimal cost for as long as needed. That would work for the short run in early spring, but the gym was not air-conditioned and the heat soon would be unbearable. Fortunately, workers were able to install units salvaged from the church. A win-win situation developed. The school now had an air-conditioned gym, and the church had a place to meet even during the hot Alabama summer.

Chris knew that the worship service on Easter would set the tone for the recovery. His message would need to be consoling and comforting, but also challenging. While he wrestled with the message he was to preach, a minister friend called, one who had been through a disastrous hurricane in Florida. His advice to Chris was to get with God and find the strength to be both assuring and at the same time transparent. It was a confirmation of what Chris already knew.

The Easter service was packed. No one counted, but a conservative estimate of the attendance was more than a thousand. Without a doubt, it was the largest crowd in the history of Bethel Baptist Church. From the front to the back, there was universal agreement that it was a worship service unlike any that the church had experienced before. Every aspect of the music, the specials, and the congregational singing "was pure celebration," Chris later reflected. It was passionate with tears flowing freely and joy abounding that a church that had seen its facilities almost completely destroyed only four days earlier was able to worship God together with praise and thanksgiving. In the sermon, Chris emphasized that no one can have all the answers in the midst of a catastrophe, but it did not matter because God had the answers. God would use this tragedy to bring triumph. God would demonstrate His restoring power in a way that would impact both the church and the community. The message was inspiring and reassuring. As never before, Bethel was reminded of the importance of worship.

The congregation had settled on a place to meet for worship, but many other details remained. Where would the nursery meet? Would Sunday school be able to meet? The need for the congregation to gather in small groups was more important than ever before. The worship services would be times of inspiration and challenge, but the small groups allowed members to experience the relational bonds that were critical to maintain in such a time of disruption. Without a vibrant Sunday school, the fringe members could slip away. The high school had a couple of rooms that the congregation could use for some of the nursery needs, but where would it find 39 Sunday school rooms? Once again, the community opened up. One after another, businesses began to offer their space. Gradually over the next few weeks, the leadership team began to obtain space for Sunday school. Classes met in banks, restaurants, professional offices, homes, and any and every place in the community. Workers brought portable buildings to the church campus for additional nursery and children's space. In nontraditional places and ways, God had provided.

Meeting the space needs involved sacrifices. Until additional portable buildings became available, the church office was in a large tent at the site of the destruction. Enduring cold spring mornings was part of the hardship. But as spring changed to summer and the immediate issues had been addressed, the harder leadership challenges began to surface. The emotional response of the first few days and weeks produced many willing workers. The long-term realities would test that commitment. Every week, volunteers had to set up and tear down for worship at the school. In addition, though space was found for all the Sunday school classes, it was not convenient. Families often had to drop off their variously aged children at different locations. What initially seemed like an adventure soon became drudgery for some. Helping people sustain the commitment and minimize grumbling required continual focus on the vision of the church. Along with this emphasis, the pastoral skills of Chris softened tensions. The staff team and leadership were successful to the point that, even in the midst of the inconvenience, attendance remained strong.

The visionary focus was also invaluable in getting through the most explosive issue the church would face during the rebuild. What should they do with the old auditorium? The church had been in two services for over a decade. There was unanimity over the need for the church to build a new worship center but not about the fate of the old building. Further complicating the issue was the settlement offer of the insurance company. The company would give the church $1.2 million in credits for whatever type of building it decided to erect, or a check for $720,000 toward the debt. The church was in a position to use the money toward an acute need, a new educational wing. The staff team and the leadership believed God was providing the funds for them to build the educational wing. They would have to incur some additional debt, but it was an opportunity they could not pass up.

Bethel Baptist Church members believed in congregational polity. However, the crisis had produced a situation that precluded congregational approval of everything in business meetings. Without a church vote, the leadership made the decision not to rebuild the old auditorium and not to accept the cash toward the debt. Some members disagreed. They believed that paying down the debt was the priority. In response, the pastor and the leadership stressed the vision and the necessity to build for those who would be coming as the church reached out to a growing community.

The congregation reached a strong consensus to build something in place of the old auditorium, but not what to build. A number of church members had ideas. A tense moment occurred when two prominent men of the congregation showed up at a deacons' meeting with plans in hand that differed significantly from the proposal of the pastor, staff, and leadership team. Chris was unaware that these men would be coming and had not heard anything of their plans. Sensing a power play, Chris met the challenge with a strong response. He told the men that they were out of order to make any presentation without having first informed the pastor, associate pastor, and other key leaders. The result was that the men backed off, and Chris's actions reaffirmed his leadership.

After three or four months, the church entered a new phase. The demolition was completed and the rubble hauled away. The role of the immediate response team was now over, and the planning and implementing reverted to the normal channels of the building committee, deacons, finance committee, and so forth. In the backdrop of this change was the congregation's ongoing processing of the grief.

> *A tense moment occurred when two prominent men of the congregation showed up at a deacons' meeting.*

Among some, the angst for the loss of the old facility manifested itself in a desire to return to as much of the pre-tornado Bethel Baptist

Church world as possible. This feeling surfaced in the discussion of the service schedule. Without on-campus facilities for worship, a Sunday night service was not feasible. Once the rebuild was complete, would the church go back to having Sunday night worship? Randy, along with others, felt that permanently eliminating the Sunday night service would allow for some much-needed new structure, particularly in the area of discipleship. Any hope of change evaporated when the subject came up in a key deacons' meeting. In deference to his pastor, Randy remained silent when some of the older deacons insisted that the Sunday night service should resume when the buildings were complete. Even as they were talking, Randy was amazed that having a Sunday night service was so important, especially considering the deacons who insisted on having it seldom attended on Sunday night.

Returning to the "Old Bethel" not only involved a return to Sunday night worship, but it also caused the issue of the Wednesday night schedule to surface. During the time of the rebuild, the staff emphasized time in prayer. Larger numbers than ever flocked to the church. Instead of having mostly Bible study with a limited prayer time that was focused mainly on individuals with physical ailments, a number of groups had extended times of prayer in the portable buildings. Chris described the atmosphere in those prayer meetings as "prayer meetings like you've not been in—in your life. I mean weeping people crying out to God." Prior to the storm, Chris had expressed the need for the church to change its Wednesday format to be more oriented to prayer rather than just another Bible study. The tornado presented an opportunity to do so. The change brought a spiritual uplift to the church. As a result, Chris was stunned that "by the time we got back in the building it was like, when are going back to Bible study on Wednesday night?" Chris became aware that the new normal of the post-tornado Bethel Baptist Church would bring new opportunities, but also that communicating this vision would be a challenge. He also realized that he and the church would continue to face many of the same obstacles that had always been present.

Beyond the Story: Leadership Lessons

Facing the Changes

More than 10 years after the tornado, Bethel Baptist Church was continuing to grow. However, the church had undergone a big change. At the end of that time, the pastor estimated that only about 30 percent of the membership present when the tornado struck was still at Bethel. Much of the loss was from the normal transition of deaths and relocations, with the latter being particularly prevalent in the rapidly growing suburban area in which Bethel Baptist Church is located. But perhaps there was something more. The church never experienced a split or anything close to it, but Bethel was not what it had been before the tornado. The storm had given an opportunity for a much better arrangement of physical space, but the buildings were only part of the change. The storm had reinforced the vision of reaching the community. The leadership of the pastor and key staff had been strongly established, which afforded them an opportunity to implement the vision in distinctly different and innovative ways.

Some of the new approaches, combined with the trauma over the loss of the "Old Bethel," created an environment to which some of the members no longer could connect. Gradually, they would leave rather than adapt. Even the staff was not immune. One key loss that occurred during the recovery was a staff member who had come shortly before the storm struck. He was to lead the recreation center which was about to be opened. Without a facility to work with for many months, the staff member found that his responsibilities had shifted greatly. The stress and change were too much. He left before the family life center opened. In retrospect, the church would have benefited from a more intentional strategy to help the membership cope with the changes brought on by the crisis. However, in the complexity and stress of the rebuild, it was difficult to anticipate the scope of this need.

In addition to the parting of many pre-storm members, the church suffered other disappointments. The loss of members contributed to slower-than-expected progress in retiring the debt. Along with the disappointment about the schedules for Sunday night and Wednesday night, other changes that the pastor and staff had hoped to see did not happen.

Despite these challenges, the church experienced healthy growth and became more effective in reaching its community.

Thriving, Not Just Surviving

Through the crisis, Bethel Baptist Church did not just survive. It thrived. In God's providence, three factors were particularly crucial. First, the church was unified and spiritually healthy going into the crisis. An extended revival that occurred a few months prior to the storm had yielded a greater sense of unity and spiritual renewal. The timing could not have been better.

Second, the staff had a complementary gift mix and modeled a healthy team approach to the lay leadership. For example, Chris excelled at communication and the therapeutic role of being a pastor. Randy excelled at administration. Neither was jealous of the other but instead enjoyed the release of being able to focus in the area of his gifts. Chris allowed Randy great freedom. Randy was fiercely loyal to his pastor and worked hard to allow Chris to be free from the details that would hinder him from fulfilling his potential in his areas of strength. The unselfishness modeled by the staff was contagious to the congregation, and the congregation exemplified it during the crisis. When Randy assembled the immediate response team, jealousy was not an issue. As a result, a number of strong, mature lay leaders stepped up to help meet the challenge of the recovery.

Third, the relationship that the church had established with its community was a godsend. If the high school and the local businesses had not allowed the church the use of their space, the church probably would not have done as well. In addition, the support from other churches and the denomination was crucial in a number of ways. Bethel Baptist Church benefited enormously from both the surrounding secular community and the faith community.

A Close Call

At 5:00 a.m. on December 3, 2008, Chris received a call he had hoped he would never get again. The message was that a tornado had hit Bethel Baptist Church a second time. Immediately, his wife exclaimed, "Oh my goodness! What are we going to do?" Chris hurried to the church. Indeed, an F1 tornado had struck the church. The main winds hit slightly to the north of where the previous tornado had struck. The area adjacent to the church bore the full force of the winds as two trailers were demolished and one house received extensive damage. There was a harrowing rescue of one person before a house collapsed, but miraculously no one was seriously hurt. The destruction to the church was not nearly as extensive as from the first storm, yet some roof structures suffered severe damage. Repair costs would total over $200,000. But through it all, Chris could breathe a sigh of relief. God once again had spared lives, and this time the congregation did not have to vacate the facilities. Bethel Baptist Church would face this and other challenges with the faith they

> *"Oh my goodness! What are we going to do?"*

had learned through overcoming the catastrophic crisis that had occurred 10 years earlier.

Questions for Further Thought

1. How did the existing leadership model at Bethel aid in coping with the crisis? In what way could it have been more effective?
2. What role did meeting that first Sunday after the storm play in establishing the new normal? What important biblical themes needed expounding in the worship and sermon the first Sunday after the storm?
3. In what ways did Randy use his development of a crisis leadership team to an advantage? What could have been some of the dangers of creating such a team? How did Randy avoid these dangers?
4. What would be some important factors in determining how the community supports a church in the midst of a crisis similar to what Bethel experienced?
5. What decisive actions did the leadership initially take that seemed to benefit the church significantly? What were the risks of these actions?

6. How did Bush and Randy have to adapt their leadership styles in dealing with the variety of challenges? How comfortable would you be in making such adjustments?
7. What old opportunities were lost because of the storm? What new opportunities did the storm create? What were the keys to taking advantage of them?
8. What were some of the leadership issues faced in working through the transitional phases?
9. In what ways did the aftermath bring about unexpected results?

Bethel's new worship center after the tornado. PHOTO BY ERIC PARSONS.

Chapter 3

God's Grace in the Midst of Grief

"Joy and gladness will overtake them, and sorrow and sigh-
ing will flee."   Isaiah 35:10b

First Baptist Church, Shreveport

The youth group of First Baptist Church, Shreveport (FBC Shreveport), Louisiana, left in its two-year-old church bus about 4:00 a.m. on Sunday, July 12, 2009. The 40-passenger bus had only 17,000 miles on it and was current with all of its maintenance. The group was headed to youth camp in Macon, Georgia, with 23 people, most of them youth and some adult leaders. Both the youth and the adult leaders had been looking forward to this day for some time.

About four hours into the trip, in Jackson, Mississippi, a second driver took a turn at the wheel. He had driven only a couple of hours, just past Meridian, Mississippi, when one of the rear tires of the church bus blew out, causing it to swerve. The bus veered so violently that a second

First Baptist Church, Shreveport. PHOTO BY KEVIN LANGLEY.

National Guardsman and rescue workers on the scene of the accident. PHOTO BY JIMMY ECKMAN.

tire blew. The driver was unable to control the vehicle, and it lurched off the pavement and rolled approximately three times. One teenage boy and two teenage girls were thrown out of the bus. When the bus came to rest, it was on top of the two girls.

Ronney Joe Webb, recreation minister at FBC was chaperoning on the trip. He called his wife to tell her about the horrifying accident. It was a little after 10:00 a.m., and Sunday school had just finished with the transition to worship just beginning. She immediately went to the activities center, where the church was holding a simultaneous worship service, and found Pastor Greg Hunt. As could be expected, she was distraught, so it took a little while for everyone to grasp what had happened. When the staff ministers and laity finally were able to absorb what was going on, they immediately had prayer and returned to the main building to locate the youth's parents and adults' families.

Gene Hendrix, the minister of education and administration, went to the sanctuary to look for John Henson, the associate pastor. John was scheduled to preach in the sanctuary service, and his daughter was on the trip. By the time Gene found Hendrix, he was on the phone with Ronney Joe getting an update from the crash site. John's daughter was among the youth who were seriously injured; a few weeks later, in a Meridian hospital, she died from her injuries.

Back at the crash site, the bus was still on its side with the two teenage girls pinned underneath. John's daughter was unresponsive and had received traumatic head injuries. The other girl apparently had cleared a window without hitting any of the framework of the bus. When people got to her, she was awake and asking for help. She knew that something was on top of her, holding her down, but she was not cognizant that it was the bus itself. All she knew was that she needed help to get this thing off her. Tragically, the teenage boy who was thrown out of the bus was pronounced dead at the scene.

A bus carrying soldiers from an Alabama National Guard unit returning from camp in Mississippi had been following the church bus a couple of vehicles behind. During their training, they had focused on emergency protocols in vehicle rollovers. Fortunately, some firefighters and nurses were part of this National Guard unit. Witnessing the church bus crash, they immediately pulled up behind the bus, and the leader of the unit ran to assess the situation. At once he waved for the rest of his unit to help, and they all hurried to the scene. The soldiers got everyone out of the bus. Seeing the girls pinned under the vehicle, the men and women in the unit lifted the bus off the kids and righted it.

> *During their training, they had focused on emergency protocols in vehicle rollovers.*

The members of the unit then set up a medical triage and prioritized those with more severe injuries to be treated and taken to the hospital first. They quickly assessed that both the girls under the bus were in trouble. These two were airlifted to a hospital in Jackson, Mississippi. Injuries for the other passengers ranged widely. One of the adult leaders suffered multiple fractures of the pelvis, ribs, and neck; a second adult experienced a cracked vertebra; and the third adult leader had a broken collar bone. The same was true for the teens—many had broken bones, and most passengers had cuts and bruises to varying degrees. Eventually, the injured received treatment at three hospitals in Meridian. Again through God's providence, just the week before the bus crash, one of these hospitals had passed the certification required to treat multiple-injury traumas. The soldiers remained until every person was handed off to emergency responders.

> *Seeing the girls pinned under the vehicle, the men and women in the unit lifted the bus off the kids and righted it.*

Some of the youth had cell phones and miraculously did not lose them in the crash. Almost immediately the calls started coming to some of the parents from their children. Information and misinformation spread through the congregation. The ministerial staff had no way of knowing what the kids had communicated. To make matters worse, the staff did not know the details of the accident. Ronney Joe, seriously injured himself, was making the primary calls to the staff. He is credited with keeping everyone calm at the crash site as well as in Shreveport via cell phone by controlling the flow of information.

Ronney Joe indicated that a few of the teenagers' parents needed to be taken aside and given the hard news of the critical condition of their children. These parents, one of them a staff member, were asked to step out to the hallway and were told the news. When a woman in the church heard of the desperate condition of the teens, she immediately stepped up to help. Her husband owned an airplane, and she volunteered the plane to fly parents to the Jackson hospital to be with their children.

The news that the teenage boy had died at the crash site came after the families were on the plane. The staff member on the plane had to break the news to that family. Everyone else went to Jackson, but this family went to Meridian. The plane landed in Jackson and dropped off the two families whose daughters were in a Jackson hospital.

As the other parents and family at FBC began to discover what had happened, amazingly most of them remained calm. Their first task was to get to the hospital. Church members began to volunteer to take parents and other relatives to be with their loved ones. Eventually a considerable caravan headed to Meridian.

Unfortunately, some parents and family in the worship service did not receive the initial word of the accident. As the sanctuary service began, Gene Hendrix announced what had happened and led in prayer. The family members who had not heard the bad news left following the prayer.

Some of the people who treated the injured in the Meridian hospitals called their churches seeking help. Three local Baptist churches immediately told their respective congregations about the accident. The churches' responses were so quick that they practically met the bus crash victims on arrival at the hospitals. The pastors and members of these three churches stayed with the youth and adults of FBC Shreveport until their families arrived. None of them were left to be by themselves. One of the pastors and some members from one of the churches went to the crash site and collected all the luggage of the FBC folks and took it to their church. Families were directed to the church to pick up the belongings after their children were released from the hospital.

The pastor of the FBC Shreveport Chinese church was the bus driver at the time of the accident. The cause of the wreck later was determined to be equipment failure. The driver, who was the least hurt, was able, with the help of the people in Meridian, to run a circuit among the three hospitals and constantly check on the FBC people.

On Monday, Gene met with four church members with unique skills and expertise who had volunteered their services. Once the news of a death in a bus wreck had reached local media, news teams began arriving at the church. Greg and Gene realized the church leadership would have to interact with the news media. Fortunately, one of the lay people had been a television news reporter for a local station. Since he knew almost everyone in the media industry in Shreveport, his assistance was invaluable. He became the media liaison for the church during this crisis. For the next couple of weeks he organized interviews with the van loads of reporters who arrived at the church. This intervention allowed the church leadership to focus on ministering to the families. He arranged interviews for the pastor to speak to the media without compromising the ministry efforts.

Another person staying after church was the chairman of deacons who was an attorney with experience in these kinds of matters. He met with Greg and Gene and provided guidance in what the church needed to do in relation to the insurance company. Additionally, he worked with the media liaison to determine the flow of information to the media. His ability to paint a picture of possible scenarios helped guide the staff through these difficult days.

Later Sunday afternoon, Greg and Gene met to assess the situation. They determined there was a need for coordinating ministry to these families and providing counseling as needed. The church staff also determined that they needed to coordinate their ministry to these families. On Monday, Gene asked one church member with whom he met whether she would take the lead in this endeavor. She organized care teams for every family affected. These teams visited each family, discovered the needs that the people of the church could meet, and then reported these needs to the coordinator. She then communicated each need to the person who could best meet that need. She coordinated the ministry of the church so that no need that could be met was left undone.

The second person Greg enlisted on Monday was a social worker who also was a great organizer. Greg enlisted her to coordinate counseling with the accident victims and family members and to deal with the calls from local churches and sister churches in every part of Louisiana who called to volunteer their services. She organized all the volunteers and counselors and arranged a meeting with all the people from the accident who were back in Shreveport. In the initial meeting, everyone who wanted to could share their feelings with the counselor and the group. This meeting was the beginning of the healing process for many of the families. In the coming weeks, FBC had two similar group meetings and also provided one-on-one counseling for those who desired it.

Beyond the Story: Leadership Lessons

Much of what is presented in this case study reflects the initial response on the day of and immediately following the bus crash. These actions were only the start of a long process. The investigation of the crash took time. The Mississippi State Police concluded that the crash was caused by equipment failure. There was no way the driver could have prevented the crash. This finding gave him some emotional relief, but there were still scars and wounds.

In the weeks following the crash, individuals in the Alabama National Guard Unit, as well as people in the three Meridian churches, continued to correspond with the members of FBC Shreveport. Some of the FBC families attended a special service to honor the National Guard Unit. The governor of Alabama presented the soldiers with a special award for their heroic service. In January 2010, the unit was deployed to Iraq, and many of the FBC families traveled to Alabama to see them off and to offer support to their families.

The initial response was critical in that it set the tone for the days ahead. The leaders were required to be both leaders and managers. Information, travel, schedules, and a host of other details had to be managed, and this required leadership. Who was to make a decision and how that decision would be made were determined as the staff responded to receiving the message from Ronney Joe's wife. They prayed and then began to notify. Although simple, their response was decisive and evidences their leadership style prior to the incident. They had roles to carry out, clearcut accountability, and a sense of team that was borne out when the pressure was on.

This case study focused mostly on the response efforts led by Greg Hunt and Gene Hendrix. However, Gene did not take over the process as other staff sat idle. The pastor carried out media interviews and led the pastoral care. There were two funerals and multiple hospitals to be visited. Gene and others enabled the pastor to meet the ministry needs. Gene's response

> *Gene's response demonstrates leadership from the second chair.*

demonstrates leadership from the second chair. By organizing the structure for response, delegating responsibilities to qualified people, and communicating insurance information to accident victims, Gene made it possible for the pastor to minister and represent God effectively in this crisis.

Often people forget about the service they could provide from the second chair because they are so focused on getting to the first chair. As important as being *the* leader is, not neglecting the support role when one is not the primary leader is just as important. Gene and the other staff members obviously made an impact through their leadership roles even though they were not carrying the title of the primary leader. Imagine the outcome if Gene had tried to move to the first chair. The desire to help people directly could have been an overwhelming temptation. However, by choosing to lead as the secondary leader, Gene was able to help more people in actual ministry, maximize ministry efforts, and provide the needed information to make well-informed decisions.

> *Often people forget about the service they could provide from the second chair because they are so focused on getting to the first chair.*

It would also have been tempting for the pastor to have taken the lead in this crisis. Most would not have thought twice about doing so in this situation. However, taking control would have gotten him bogged down in details that would have been unable to provide the ministry care and personal response required. Trusting ministry to the enlisted volunteers allowed both Greg and Gene to provide leadership in their areas of the response effort.

Communication was critical during this crisis. Parents and family members needed to be notified. Travel arrangements had to be secured. Insurance companies had to be contacted. Ministry needs had to be directed to persons able to meet them. Information and misinformation had to be sifted and media briefings coordinated and prepared for. Although what and how something was said was important, in this situation the system for saying it was just as important. When a need was expressed, a system had to be in place for the receiver of that information to pass it on to the appropriate person who could then act. In some ways, a clear system for communication was more important than the information.

One of the communication issues faced early on was notifying families. Some were notified personally, whereas others heard through the grapevine or general announcements. Mobile devices only added to the challenge. Misinformation and misunderstanding increased because so much information was coming without any filters. Unknowingly, Ronney Joe became the filter that brought structure to the communication barrage. The issue was not information, but rather reliable information. Creating such a communication filter is important to any organization if the leaders are going to be able to make well-informed decisions.

Greg and Gene organized an initial response and, in turn, trusted others to assist them in the process. Regardless of the organization, trust is essential for leadership to take place. After Greg and Gene had established a process, Greg trusted Gene with its implementation while he was involved in direct pastoral ministry to victims. Gene had to feel that he was trusted or, instead of acting decisively, he would have been second guessing his decision while implementing it, which is a bad place for any leader to be. Because he was trusted, he could empower others with that same kind of trust and enable them to act with confidence as well.

Trust has to be fostered and earned, especially in local congregations. In most church settings, the congregation has seen pastors and other staff members come and go. Some they wanted to see go, and others they did not. When a new staff member arrives, he or she must begin immediately to build trust. By studying hard, seeking wise counsel, and honestly praying for and following God's counsel, the staff members can build trust effectively. Trust is the equity for leadership. If a group trusts the leader and his or her judgment, they will be more willing to follow when difficult decisions are faced.

> *Trust has to be fostered and earned, especially in local congregations.*

Every leadership crisis involves some form of God's sovereignty. In this crisis, the bus of National Guardsmen and the hospitals just receiving training point to God's sovereign grace. These circumstances were not accidental or coincidental. The resources at Greg and Gene's disposal were not coincidental either. They realized that God was showing His grace even in the midst of a tragedy. We often forget that God allows us to be in the right place at the right time with the right tools to make a difference. We are too quick to take the credit and forget that every contact and relationship is a gift from God.

> *. . . the staff members can build trust effectively.*

Within God's sovereignty we discover that God could choose another person to carry the burden of leadership in that crisis. There may be people more qualified, but God did not place them in that chair at that time. He put you there. Perhaps he chose you for such a time as this (see Esth 4:14). This reality should drive each of us to thank God humbly for the opportunity and then continually point others to Him as an act of worship.

Youth prayer wall after the accident. PHOTO BY KEVIN LANGLEY.

Questions for Further Thought

1. How could communication have been improved in this situation? What mechanisms do you have in place for ensuring clear communication?
2. Identify the contacts and networks that were used to respond to this crisis. What role did the network play in the response? What networks are you fostering that could be called on in a crisis?
3. What things are you doing to build trust? How could the things you do today add to or subtract from the trust required for you to lead in the future?
4. In what ways did the initial response set the tone for the long-term response? What actions in the initial response point to a greater leadership principle(s)? How can you incorporate that principle(s) into your leadership toolbox?
5. How would you describe the difference between managing and leading? How are they the same? How are they different? What actions taken by Greg and Gene would illustrate each according to your definition?

Reunion of National Guard unit with members of FBC Shreveport. PHOTO BY KEVIN LANGLEY.

Chapter 4

The Church as Family

"When the foundations are destroyed, what can the righteous do?"
Psalm 11:3

First Baptist Church, Maryville

Sunday, March 8, 2009, began a little differently for Rich Cochran. He had been minister of education at FBC Maryville, Illinois, for only a short time. His day started at the airport, greeting a ministerial staff candidate and his wife. Cochran and his guests arrived at the church around 8:15, when the first morning worship service began. As Rich walked past the sanctuary doors, he noticed attendance was low. That day in the 8:15 service, fewer than 90 people were present, mainly because of the time change. Rich walked the ministerial staff candidate through the building, introducing him to the first-hour Sunday school teachers. The candidate's wife went in the nursery for a few minutes. During the brief tour, Rich was approached by one of the church members. As he addressed this individual, the ministerial candidate proceeded to the nursery to join his wife. At about 8:45 a.m., Rich returned to the nursery to pick up the

First Baptist Church, Maryville. PHOTO BY ERIN WESTFALL.

candidate and his wife. The candidate was to be introduced in all three morning services. As Rich made his way to the nursery, he heard a gunshot, quickly followed by a few more shots. Rich knew, because of the loudness of the shots, that the sound resonated from within the building.

Terry Joe Sedlacek had walked in to the first of the three scheduled worship services and proceeded to the platform where Pastor Fred Winters was preaching. Pastor Fred responded, "Brother, can I help you?"

> *Melton and Terry Bullard rushed to rescue Pastor Fred as he and Sedlacek struggled on the floor.*

At that, Sedlacek pulled out a handgun and fired four shots at Pastor Fred. In his account afterward, Keith Melton noted that Pastor Fred acted heroically in attempting to keep the gunman from firing on the congregation, and that as a result the gun jammed.[1] Melton and Terry Bullard rushed to rescue

Pastor Fred as he and Sedlacek struggled on the floor. Both Melton and Bullard received stab wounds as they sought to subdue Sedlacek. Winters was mortally wounded. The congregation sat paralyzed with shock.[2]

Since Rich was in close proximity, he ran into the sanctuary. When he got there, the perpetrator was already down. Rich immediately ran back out of the sanctuary and called 911. He was asked to stay on the line and speak with the police. Following the call, he hurried back into the sanctuary to try to make out what was happening. At this point, he had no idea that Pastor Fred had been shot.

Pastor Fred Winters family. PHOTO BY KAREN LYNCH.

Rich concentrated on helping congregants to remain calm as he attempted to assess the situation. While a few of the worshippers had walked out to the foyer, the church leadership made an effort to keep the congregants from leaving the sanctuary. They knew the fewer people who moved, the better this situation could be handled. They also needed to keep the congregants where they were to obtain their statements of what had occurred. Everything was happening so quickly.

The police arrived soon after Rich's call. Rich ran out to the front of the facilities trying to catch the police and the ambulance so that he could usher them into the sanctuary quickly. As Rich accompanied the police and EMT to the front of the sanctuary, the commotion and blood made it impossible for him to determine who had been shot. As he peered over the nurses who were in attendance in the church service, he asked who had been shot. They responded, "It is Pastor Fred." Rich tried desperately to get close enough and to say a prayer for him.

Rich was not sure whether his pastor was still alive at that point. He realized his mood would be contagious, so he tried to remain as calm as possible so the people in the sanctuary could sense a degree of peace in a chaotic situation. Melton and Bullard, who had come to the aid of Pastor Fred, needed to be treated for their stab wounds. The police secured the building, and the ambulance took Pastor Fred to the hospital. Bullard's father and two other church members picked up Bullard, dragged him out to a personal vehicle, and took him to the hospital. He was airlifted to a hospital in St. Louis that was better equipped to deal with his injury. Had he not been transferred, Bullard likely would have bled to death. Melton, who was taken to a local hospital, was treated and released that day. Sedlacek also was taken to a hospital where he remained for some time.

Some of the police remained in the building, sequestering the congregants who had been eyewitnesses to the shooting, standard operating procedure so as not to taint the statements of the witnesses with outside influences. Only 40 minutes had gone by before Rich received a call on his cell phone from Fox News. To this day he has no idea how they got his number. Rich told Fox News that he was not making any statements at that time. One of the Illinois Baptist State Association (IBSA) staff members was at FBC Maryville to speak to a group of youth. When he became aware of what had occurred and the need to interact with the media, he sent an e-mail to his colleague Marty King, the IBSA communication director. Marty's expertise was invaluable—he spent the afternoon filtering phone calls, taking notes, coaching Rich and the church leaders on what to say and what not to say and what to expect in a press conference, and giving other specific direction to handle the situation.

During this entire time Rich and the other church leaders did not know the extent or outcome of Pastor Fred's injuries. Even so, because of the wide use of cell phones and smart phones, the congregants already were receiving text messages indicating Pastor Fred was dead. Misinformation seemed to be the norm. Some sent e-mails to Cindy Carnes, the pastor's assistant, saying they had heard Pastor Fred had died. Rich had not been informed of Pastor Fred's condition and, consequently, could not confirm or deny this statement. Rich went to the police chief, who was on site, and asked whether he could confirm the rumor that Pastor Fred had died. This was one of the most difficult things Rich had to do. Pulling him aside, the police chief confirmed Pastor Fred had died but told Rich he could not share this information with anyone to avoid influencing the statements of the witnesses. However, the police chief gave Rich permission to tell Cindy, and Mark Jones, the worship pastor.

> *Rich felt competing loyalties regarding the congregation. He wanted to be loyal to Pastor Fred in pursuit of his murderer, but he also felt the need to share this information with the congregation Pastor Fred loved so dearly.*

Rich felt competing loyalties regarding the congregation. He wanted to be loyal to Pastor Fred to build a case against his murderer, but he also felt the need to share this information with the congregation that Pastor Fred loved so dearly. Not until four hours later—at around

1:30 p.m.—did the police allow Rich to tell the church family that Pastor Fred had passed away.

After sharing this information, Rich and Mark knew they needed to call the congregation back together that evening. However, their sanctuary was a crime scene and the police were not going to release the building until it was processed for evidence. Rich sent one of the church staff members to a church down the road to talk with their pastor about using their building for the evening. This church graciously turned over its building to FBC Maryville. They spent all afternoon creating overflow seating, which facilitated FBC coming together as a body in the middle of their pain. Understandably, Pastor Fred's wife and children did not attend.

During that night's service the congregation sang four or five songs, and Mark spoke about the promises of heaven. Rich spoke about Pastor Fred's mission, how he lived his life, and what he would expect from the church. Even so, prayer was the main focus, and the service served as a rallying cry for the challenging days ahead. The people needed a focus. Even amid the grief and tears of this church family, Rich knew someone needed to say there is a tomorrow and to lead them to walk through this tragedy. That Sunday evening was a critical time. Hope and peace were offered in the midst of so many unknowns.

> *Rich remembers telling his wife he wished he could just step to the edge of the platform in the sanctuary and assure his church everything was going to be okay and to offer some hope in the middle of all of the craziness.*

Before Rich could go home, he held a press conference and spoke to numerous people. Throughout this tragedy and as he cared for his church and handled the media, Rich maintained great control and composure. He did not allow himself to feel the events of the day. Not until 11:00 that night, when he lay in bed with his wife, did he allow the tragedy of that day to sink in. Finally allowing himself to rest, all Rich could do was cry. The safety of being with his wife at home gave Rich the permission not to be the one who was in charge, but to lean on his wife for comfort and support. Rich remembers telling his wife he wished he could just step to the edge of the platform in the sanctuary and assure his church everything was going to be okay and to offer some hope in the middle of all of the craziness.

Monday was a whirlwind. At 5:00 that morning Rich went from being an ordinary minister of education to appearing on *Good Morning America*, *Fox and Friends*, and several other media outlets. After dividing their time between the national press agencies, Rich and Mark made their way to the downtown St. Louis hospital to see Terry Bullard. Although he eventually would recover fully, at that point he was in critical condition. By 9:00 a.m. both Rich and Mark were back in their respective offices at the church. They were met with ringing phones and church members desiring to serve in the church as a way to work out their grief. Rich and the other staff members were not sure what to do, but they decided to give people work to do in the church facilities. Many took upon themselves the cleaning of the church. Rich recalls thinking they were going to have the cleanest church in America. The people just wanted to be in the church. Even in the midst of the craziness, the church campus— the crime scene—was the safe haven. The congregation wanted to be in God's house. FBC Maryville's maintenance team turned the building over to Rich and the other staff members. By Monday the church members had cut out the carpet, patched up the spots where bullet holes remained, and painted. The immediacy of attending to these things was essential, as the congregation wanted to be back in the sanctuary to pray.

Billy Graham's Rapid Response Team, who had called Sunday afternoon offering to help, arrived on Tuesday following the shooting. Rich recalls what a gift from God this team was as their counselors effectively ministered to and counseled the staff and congregants of FBC Maryville. While many people did not feel they needed this counseling, Rich knew he did. To this day Rich is not sure how he would have walked through this time had it not been for this caring team. In addition, staff from the Baptist Children's Home came to minister and offer assistance.

Pastor Fred's visitation was scheduled for Thursday with the funeral the next day. Rich guessed 7,000 to 10,000 people attended the visitation alone. Pastor Fred had led this church for 22 years, and the attendance had grown from fewer than 200 to more than 1,400. He had been a pastor in every sense of the word—personable and genuine, truly shepherding his people.

Cindy, Pastor Fred's wife, and their children were given time alone with their husband and father's body at 1:30 p.m. prior to the visitation. The staff joined Cindy and the children at 2:00 p.m., when public visitation began. Rich had the privilege of standing next to either Cindy or her parents at the edge of the casket and greeting church members who had come to pay their respects. As Rich stood at the family's side, God gave him his heart's desire by letting the congregation know everything was going to be all right. Rich felt as if God tapped him on the shoulder and said, "I gave you your wish of telling everyone it was going to be okay." Instead of standing at the edge of the platform in the sanctuary and speaking to the congregation, Rich was able to comfort each individual personally.

> *Rich felt as if God tapped him on the shoulder and said, "I gave you your wish of telling everyone it was going to be okay."*

On Friday, the family and community celebrated the life and ministry of Dr. Fred Winters. Dr. Al Meredith had called on the day after the shooting and made himself available to help in whatever way was needed. Dr. Meredith had been the pastor at Wedgewood Baptist in Fort Worth, Texas, when a gunman entered the sanctuary and shot several congregants. Thus, he was uniquely capable of empathizing with the situation that First Baptist Church, Maryville was facing. Mark and Rich decided to call Dr. Meredith, and on Saturday he graciously came to Maryville to meet with the leaders and staff, giving wisdom and comfort as well as filling the pulpit on Sunday.

On Sunday morning, Rich arrived at 7:30. As he pulled into the church's driveway, he was surprised to see policemen from more than

35 departments lining the entrances to the church. He thought, "Oh no, not again." As it turned out, these officers were sent as a demonstration of the community's support, respect, and tribute to Pastor Fred and First Baptist Church, Maryville. The church was overwhelmed. Dr. Meredith was able to minister to the church in a way that only someone who has walked the same path could. The Lord was present in every way. More than 500 people were in attendance at the first service that Sunday morning. Additionally, on this first Sunday the total attendance at all three services was 2,000, whereas the average was 1,450. FBC Maryville could not—and did not—walk this journey alone. Through the help and guidance of many individuals, the church was able to come out on the other side strong. FBC Maryville continues to grow today.

Beyond the Story: Leadership Lessons

Rich, Mark, and the church leaders faced several challenges as they began to respond to this terrible day. Everything included in the story described above took place in one week. On their calendars were other things they had planned to do, but those activities were suddenly obsolete.

Through God's grace, Pastor Fred's family was spared the horror and grief of witnessing their husband and father attacked and mortally wounded. This was not the only blessing in an otherwise horrendous crisis. Although the event was tragic, no other church staff or lay leader was fatally injured. Additionally, neither Mark nor Rich was in the sanctuary to witness the attack. Their absence gave them a spiritual and psychological advantage so they could provide the leadership required in this crisis. Rich was able to protect his own family from this chaos by calling his wife and asking her to stay home with their children.

Altogether, these seemingly small details enabled Rich and the other staff to focus on the situation at hand. Undivided attention and concentration were essential. Leadership always requires clarity, especially in a crisis. Many decisions needed to be made, the first of which was what to do about the rest of the day.

The Holy Spirit directed their hearts to a time of prayer just as steel is drawn to a magnet. Rich and Mark knew that corporate prayer not only would begin the healing but would also provide much-needed direction and comfort for the challenging days that lay ahead. Accordingly, they secured a neighboring church, and the church family met there the Sunday evening of Pastor Fred's murder.

This time may have been more important for the staff than for the members. Had they not had the service, the staff most likely would have found a way to gather and grieve with one another. However, this assembly gave them the opportunity to grieve with the church and set the tone for the next steps. As they grieved together, the staff and members were able to move forward together. They needed each other, and this was a first step in building that interdependency.

Rick immediately recognized that neither he nor anyone else at First Baptist Church was in a position to handle the magnitude of the emotional trauma the congregation had experienced. Once again the Lord's hand was evident in this situation. Both Rich and Mark were open and eager to accept the help of so many ministry colleagues from across the country who offered their assistance.

Although Rich was spared witnessing the tragedy of his pastor's murder and his congregants' injury, he carried the emotional wounds of the tragedy. This weight was magnified by the need to suppress his emotions for the benefit of his church family. Rich realized that in order to minister properly to his church family and his own family, he had to avail himself of the counseling offered by the Billy Graham Response Team. Rich recalled, "Spending thirty minutes with their counselor was probably the best thing I did that week."

Often the needs of the one ministering are neglected, especially in these types of crises. Remember, Rich was a coworker and had lost the person who had given him direction and counsel. We cannot ignore our own needs during a crisis. Too many times, ministers suppress their feelings and never allow themselves to be human. Doing so often leads to physical or emotional problems and burnout. Leadership is not about functioning above the problem. It is about functioning within the problem.

Fred had done a masterful job establishing a leadership team in good times. He established deacons who did what deacons were supposed to do—serve. He provided the freedom for his staff to function within their roles. He encouraged the church family to lead in service. This preparation was invaluable in leading through the crisis. Despite the chaos, members knew the roles they were to fulfill. Rich reflected on the pastor's leading of the church in his own personal ministry: "[It] wasn't the first time you were stepping into these shoes and going, 'Now what in the world do I do?'" Pastor Fred had allowed his staff to serve in instrumental leadership roles, thereby preparing them to take the helm. He had afforded this opportunity to the lay leaders as well, which helped them formulate a leadership strategy. Thus, the church was able to address the challenges it faced in the months following the death of their pastor. Security, media scrutiny as the story continued, and the securing of a new pastor were addressed with a sense of strategy because of the groundwork done by Pastor Fred.

> *Pastor Fred had allowed his staff to serve in instrumental leadership roles, thereby preparing them to take the helm.*

We may not like to hear it, but there will be a day in all our lives when we are no longer the leaders. That day may or may not come as a result of our own choosing, and we cannot predict when it will happen; but it will happen. The true test of any leader is not what happens when he or she is leading, but rather what happens when he or she is no longer the leader. Investing so others can build on your work in the future is how great organizations are built. In some ways, Fred Winters had a greater impact after his death because he had made an investment in creating an organization that could function well beyond him.

Questions for Further Thought

1. How would you describe the initial response of Rich and the other leaders?
2. What attitudes toward leadership had been fostered in Rich that enabled him to respond the way he did during that first week?
3. What does this case study reveal about the leadership of Pastor Fred? How did his investment in others enable the church he had led to move forward after his death?

4. What were the key factors that enabled the church to make such a positive impact in the midst of such a terrible tragedy?

5. What type of investment are you making in the future of the organization you now lead? What are you doing to prepare the organization to function after you have left that group, regardless of the circumstances?

Notes

1. F. Winters, *Reflections on Wisdom and Folly*, ed. C. Winter (Bloomington, IN: CrossBooks, 2010), 1.

2. See E. Roach, M. King, and L. Sergent, *Baptist Press* and the *Illinois Baptist* news journal, March 9 and 10, 2009.

Chapter 5

Beauty out of Ashes

*"To provide for those who mourn in Zion; to give them
a crown of beauty instead of ashes."*   Isaiah 61:3a

Ashby Baptist Church

"Brother Jim! The church is on fire!" came the voice of the deacon over the phone line. For the previous two years, Dr. Jim Parker had served as the bivocational pastor of Ashby Baptist Church near Montevallo, Alabama. The church was located at the juncture of three counties—Bibb, Shelby, and Chilton—and was a member of the Bibb Baptist Association. Ashby Baptist Church averaged about 135 in attendance on Sunday morning. Jim remembers thinking before he answered the early-morning phone call that calls at that time of day are rarely good news, but this Friday the news was particularly dreadful. Jim immediately asked the deacon where in the building the fire was located, and was told that it already had broken through the roof in one area. Jim first thought that perhaps part of the heating equipment had malfunctioned and started the fire.

Ashby Baptist Church before the fire. PHOTO BY JIM PARKER.

Jim and his wife Donna began the 30-mile drive to the church on what seemed to be one of the foggiest mornings he had experienced. While driving, Jim kept imagining what could have caused the fire. The last couple of miles Jim could smell the burning church building as the smoke mixed with the fog. Jim knew the fire had gotten much worse since the phone call.

The church grounds were carved out of the forest and were just like a sanctuary; the setting was beautiful. When Jim and Donna approached the church building, its shady lane, normally tranquil, was lit up from the fire. One of the church members, Billy Joe, stopped Jim and told him he had just heard that another church in the community was on fire. The news was the first indication that there was more to the fire than faulty heating equipment: *arson* crossed Jim's mind.

Jim stopped his car some distance from the church, got out, and asked whether anyone had the names and phone numbers of anyone who was affiliated with the other churches in the community. They began to call members of other congregations to warn them of possible arson and that their churches might be targeted as well. By then it was 5:15 a.m., and one of Ashby Baptist Church's members woke up one of the deacons in a neighboring church. The deacon lived near his church, so he jumped out of bed and ran over to check on the church buildings. He saw a vehicle leaving the parking lot and was able to get a description of it. When he entered the sanctuary, it was just beginning to burn. Fortunately, he was able to put out the fire and save the sanctuary with just minor damage.

By the time Jim arrived at the church, two fire departments had responded: the local volunteer fire department and the Montevallo Fire Department (MVFD). Jim and his congregants stood by helplessly as the firefighters did their dangerous work. However, even from their safe vantage point Jim and the others could see where someone had kicked in the door. The glass on the floor inside the room indicated that the building had been broken into. Jim and the church leaders realized their suspicions of arson were correct and the fires had been set on purpose.

Suddenly, a section of roof collapsed and fell onto one of the firemen, who was brought out of the burning church by the other fire fighters. Ironically, the fireman himself was an Ashby Baptist Church member, and Jim and the congregants quickly administered first aid. The section of roof had fallen on his head and injured his spine. He was taken to the hospital and later would recover from his injuries, but of course everyone was greatly concerned. An MVFD fireman cut his hand badly and was treated on site.

The sanctuary building was engulfed in fire, so the church members could not get into the buildings to salvage anything. This church had been a postcard setting. The sanctuary had been built at the turn of the twentieth century and had been remodeled several times. It was made of heart pine. When the education wing and a subsequent

> *Everything had burned.*

addition were built, the contractor inserted a connector link between the sanctuary and the new buildings as a fire stop. Without the connector link, the fire could have easily spread and burned the additions. However, the arsonists set the sanctuary on fire and then went into the education building and set it on fire as well. Everything had burned—the fire was so hot that even the metal chairs had melted.

The fire finally was extinguished, and everyone was exhausted. Jim and Donna had thrown on clothes and gotten to the church as quickly as they could following the early-morning phone call. Now they were wet, tired, and emotionally drained. They needed to get out of the weather. There was a café near the church, so Jim and Donna went there to get some coffee and warm up. The first indication that the news media had any interest in the fire came when one of the local news stations telephoned Jim at the café. He told the reporter where the church was located and that the building and contents had been a total loss. Jim also mentioned that he had been informed of the other church fires.

It was only 8:00 a.m., but by this time five churches had been set on fire and three of them, including Ashby Baptist Church, had been burned to the ground. All were Southern Baptist churches. One of them, Pleasant Sabine Baptist Church, was a dually aligned National Baptist church. Their pastor was Robert Murphy, a boyhood friend with whom Jim had played high school sports. They knew each other very well.

Returning to the church campus and driving up the shady lane toward the buildings, Jim saw in the right-hand ditch a couple of men wearing jackets with ATF (Alcohol, Tobacco, and Firearms) on the back. On the other side was a man with FBI on his jacket. In the church yard, Jim was met by one of the ATF agents and another FBI agent. When Jim asked the agents what was going on, they said only that they were there to investigate. As it turned out, about 12 federal agents and some arson investigators were already on site.

Then the news trucks from the media began to arrive. Jim was surprised to see an NBC media truck from Atlanta because the church was so close to Birmingham. Then, seemingly all at once, news outlets of every description began to pour in from everywhere: FOX News, CNN, NBC, CBS, ABC, and NPR Radio. The media would become one of the great challenges for Jim and the other church leaders to manage.

Later that day a very significant thing happened to Jim. Hank Irwin, a state senator who lived near the church and was a good friend of Jim's, came to the church when he heard about the fire. He took Jim aside and said, "Brother Jim, you are going to be thrust onto a national pulpit by the media, and it is going to give you a chance to speak for the Lord." Jim remembers how that "scared me to death." A few hours later, Jim went off by himself to be with the Lord in prayer. Hank's words were still ringing in Jim's ears, and he needed direction from God. Jim felt the Lord speak to him in a powerful way, confirming what Hank had told him only hours before. Jim thought, "Oh Lord, this is crazy here. There are things spinning around these fires that I don't understand." Jim clearly heard God speak and say, "I want you to start immediately talking about forgiving the people who did this." That word from God would shape the way Jim and the church handled the rest of this crisis.

> *"Brother Jim, you are going to be thrust onto a national pulpit by the media, and it is going to give you a chance to speak for the Lord."*

At about 10:00 a.m. that Friday, Jim gathered all the church leaders at the home of one of the deacons to meet for the first time since the fire. As they discussed what had happened, they discovered four other churches also had been burned to some degree that day. Ashby Baptist Church was the second one set on fire that day and the largest of the five; it was also larger than the four other Alabama churches that were burned in the following days. In fact, Ashby Baptist Church had been enjoying dramatic growth. The church leaders at the meeting could not help but recall that only two weeks before, the church had met to discuss building an addition to accommodate the growth. The leaders at the deacon's house decided to hold services at a sister church, Shady Grove Baptist, which had offered them space. It was nearby, located just a few miles down the road from their church site. They worked out a schedule with Shady Grove so that they could meet. Jim and many of the church members stayed all day and into the night on that dreadful Friday. Turning their attention toward the slew of media and law enforcement officers, they began trying to organize to minister to their needs for water, food, and restroom facilities.

Saturday morning, Jim got back to the church about 6 a.m. and interviewed with the *Today Show* on NBC. While doing the interview, he recalled his conversation with Hank and the message of forgiveness God had given him the day before. Jim spoke with confidence and told the reporter, "We don't know who did it, but God knows who did it. And as far as we are concerned we have forgiven these folks already. We are moving on." This interview was the first of many that allowed Jim to deliver the message of the forgiveness God had instructed him to give.

The next few days were filled with working with the insurance companies and attempting to restore some semblance of normality. The church held worship services at the Shady Grove Baptist Church building and tried to adjust to the new schedule. On Saturday, Governor Bob Riley arrived at the church site to visit Jim and provide encouragement, and on Sunday afternoon the president of the Southern Baptist Convention, Bobby Welch, stopped by to offer his prayer and support. These prayers and words of encouragement were much appreciated and very helpful.

The media were everywhere, and as time passed Jim and Ashby Baptist Church seemed to become the representatives for all the churches that had been burned. Jim, being bivocational, owned and operated a business with a partner. The media called Jim constantly at his business, at home, and on his cell phone. He could not escape them. When they called Jim asking for an interview, he would respond by saying he was unavailable at that moment, so they would wait outside or stop him on the driveway. Scheduling the media interviews became a major chore.

Throughout this media blitz, Jim remembered that God had told him to give a message of forgiveness. However, God also used this media attention to throw a spotlight on Jim's childhood friend Robert Murphy and Pleasant Sabine Baptist Church. Although Ashby Baptist Church was fully insured for replacement, his friends at Pleasant Sabine and some of the other churches did not have any insurance. Being able to get in front of the media was helpful to raise money for some of these churches.

During this time the search for the arsonists was in full swing. The Justice Department met with the leaders of the churches and decided to declare the arsons a federal crime. The U.S. Attorney in Birmingham also met with leaders and told them what the penalties would be when the criminals were caught. There were 120 federal agents on the ground investigating these church fires. It was one of the largest federal task forces that had ever been put on the ground in the history of Alabama. In just over 30 days, there were more than 600 leads that developed. Because of Jim's exposure through the media, over 60 of these leads came directly to him. These leads were from people who did not want to go to the FBI or ATF for whatever reason, and that, while in and of itself a good thing, began to take a lot of time.

In the beginning, the authorities thought a hate group may have been responsible for the crimes. Hate groups were known to meet in the area, and with Jim's personal ties with Robert at Pleasant Sabine Baptist Church, the leadership of the churches and friends began to have serious concerns for Jim's safety. The rationale was that if someone would go so far as to burn churches, then the leaders in those churches were not safe either. Jim had a security detail following him for the next few weeks. Even his business partner called Jim on his cell phone every 30 minutes to check on him.

The authorities arrested the three young men responsible for the arsons. Jim found out when he received a call from the news media asking him whether he would like to comment on the arrests. Jim responded by saying, "I don't know anything about the arrests." The news media informed Jim that three college students had been arrested. The young men were all from middle-class families and were all students at a Christian university in Birmingham. The reporter asked Jim whether he was glad, and Jim answered, "Yes, we are glad we know who was responsible, but this is one of the saddest days of my life because I understand what is going to fall on these three young men." Jim knew what these young men were facing from his previous meetings with government officials, and was surprised that he felt so distressed when he heard the news of their arrests. He had thought that it might bring closure, but it seemed only to move the events into another phase.

The week after the young men were arrested, Jim received a call from the dean of the chapel at the Christian university where the young men had been students. He told Jim that the school was going to hold a service for the three because they had been so well known. The dean also invited Jim to speak. That was the first indication to Jim that the message of forgiveness that God had given to him on the day of the fire was being heard and believed. When Jim arrived, he was surprised to hear that the parents and families of the arrested men were in attendance.

Jim spoke the message of forgiveness to the attendees of the chapel service, and following the service Jim was about to leave when a man stopped him and introduced himself as an attorney who represented one of the families; just then another man stepped up beside him and said he represented another of the families; and then an additional man said he represented the last of the families. Together they asked whether Jim would be willing to speak with them and their families. Jim agreed.

Jim remembers that meeting well, "You would expect it from the mothers, but each of the dads, in turn, came one at a time and just fell on me weeping and asking for forgiveness for their son." After they had talked awhile some of the students gathered around Jim and prayed and pledged their support to all the churches and to the young men now in jail. Jim was about to leave for the second time when one of the lawyers came back to Jim, indicating his client had asked Jim for something else. He continued, "I hope you don't think I am imposing, but my client has asked if you would be willing to speak to their sons." Jim said he would be more than glad to meet with them, but they were in custody. Jim later mentioned it to the church and told them about the chapel service. The church began to pray that he would have that opportunity.

> *Jim remembers that meeting well, "You would expect it from the mothers, but each of the dads, in turn, came one at a time and just fell on me weeping and asking for forgiveness for their son."*

Jim knew that once a person is in the custody of the federal marshall he or she isn't allowed contact with anybody; the only exception is the person's lawyer. Just when it seemed that Jim wasn't going to be allowed to meet with the young men, on the day of the arraignment Jim was invited to meet for 15 minutes with each of them. They wanted to tell

Jim what had happened and what events had led up to the burning of the churches.

Throughout Jim's conversation with the young men, he noticed that they were very remorseful. They had realized immediately that they had committed a terrible crime. They were on academic scholarship, and all had promising careers awaiting them after college. Now those careers were the last thing on anyone's mind. Jim was deeply saddened that young men who had been given a great opportunity to have a prosperous life had potentially ruined it with these dimwitted crimes. Jim told them that he and the church forgave them.

Not only did God work through the forgiveness Jim and the church lavished on these young men, but God also provided for the material needs for Ashby Baptist Church in due time. The Alabama Baptist Convention provided portable units for the congregation to hold services for the next three years and six months. During this time the church felt God leading them to relocate. A local resident would later donate 10 acres of land for the new church site, confirming this decision. An architect from Boston, Massachusetts, volunteered his services to the church, and designed a wonderful structure. The church held their first service in the new building on January 3, 2010.

Beyond the Story: Leadership Lessons

Jim did not let his fear of the tasks ahead paralyze him from being faithful to these tasks. Rather, he seized the opportunity to use every means of communication available to him, including interpersonal relationships and news media, to proclaim the message God told him to proclaim—God's forgiveness.

No one would have blamed Jim or his church members if they had been angry with the young men who set the fire. Through God's power, Jim and his congregation were able to forgive these young men for their careless acts. The role that Jim played in this was crucial. He set the tone for how everyone else responded. Had he celebrated the arrests, others would have followed suit. Instead, he responded with empathy and sadness. His response demonstrated a maturing portrait of sin and its consequences in our world.

When given the opportunity to bring ministry and healing to the families through the act of forgiveness, Jim also freely extended God's love through his own words of reconciliation. He became the spokesman who freed everyone else to forgive. When things like this happen, it would be easy for a person to become vengeful and angry. However, that usually leads only to bitterness and dissatisfaction. Leaders who harbor the pain of being victims will continue to lead, but not in a way that pleases God or benefits His kingdom. Jim's desire to please God trhough this experience is evident by his expressions of forgiveness.

> *Leaders who harbor the pain of being a victim will continue to lead, but they will not do so in a way that pleases God or benefits His kingdom. Jim's desire to please God though this experience is evident by his expressions of forgiveness.*

There had been all kinds of theories for the arsons; but it turned out that on the night of the first five fires, the young men had been night hunting—poaching deer. They had been drinking alcohol and smoking marijuana and decided to break in to the first church as a prank, not intending to do harm. After they were finished looking around in the church they began to worry that the police were going to collect their DNA and they would be caught. These worries seemed to come from television shows.

They grabbed the silk flowers from the Lord's Supper table and set them on fire in the middle of the floor of the sanctuary and left. After having driven a short distance, they looked back and could see a fireball in the sky. Realizing the seriousness of their actions, and the fact they had to drive past the building to escape, they were afraid of being found out. By that time, people were gathering to help put out the fire, and the young men thought they had been spotted. In order to throw off the authorities and avoid being caught, they burned the other churches. All the other arsons had been an attempt to cover up their first church fire.

Their lack of judgment made it more important for Jim to demonstrate fairness and sound judgment. He demonstrated how a true leader makes a decision. While he may react, he does so not for self-preservation but out of principle. Jim responded this way. That is why it is so important for leaders to develop firm beliefs and to live with confidence in those beliefs. When the crisis comes, the leader does not then need to decide what he will do and what he believes. Instead, he or she has to decide only what will be done based on sure beliefs.

Jim's experience also demonstrates that bivocational ministry is not the same as part-time ministry. Although these were difficult days for Jim and his family, he maintained his responsibility at his business while being available to the needs of his congregation and the perpetrators and their families to bring about restoration. Jim did not allow the craziness of his schedule and the fact he was not a full-time pastor to dictate how he would conduct his ministry and care for the people involved.

Jim's business partner played a significant role in this process. He did not abandon Jim, nor did he forget to be empathetic. His understanding and concern for Jim were a source of encouragement. Even if we are not the one directly impacted, we can make a difference. Our expressions of concern, offers to help, and phone calls about the normal duties of life (in Jim's case, the regular business operations) can bring balance and perspective.

Even in the midst of the crisis, Jim took time to focus on God. That decision alone was the critical step that made it possible for Jim to lead his church and community through this crisis. It is so easy for us to focus on the immediate need and move to response mode without consulting God first. We may think there is no time, but the truth is there is no better time. The comfort and message given to him by God in that moment drove Jim's decisions and determined how he responded to the media, to the arrested students, and to the community.

Questions for Further Thought

1. What factors cause us to look to our own understanding instead of turning to God first when facing a crisis?

2. If the community in which you lead were to adopt your attitude, would that be a good thing or bad thing? Why?

3. Jim already had the respect and trust of many in his community or he would not have been able to assume the role of speaker for the community. What are you doing to make yourself a worthy spokesperson for your community? How are you building respect and trust?

4. What role did being a bivocational pastor play in this crisis? How was it a hindrance? How was it an asset?

5. How could Jim have managed the phone calls more efficiently? How important was it for Jim to manage his time during this period? What time-management habits are you developing that could be helpful when you face a crisis?

Ashby Baptist Church after the fire. PHOTO BY JIM PARKER.

Ashby Baptist Church rebuilt. PHOTO BY DEBBIE C. SWEET.

PART II

The Crushing Unexpected

Chapter 6

When Trust Is Lost

"Strike the shepherd, and the sheep will be scattered."
Zechariah 13:7

First Baptist Church, Oak Forest

John Robertson was glad finally to have some down time. He had been in the ministry for a more than 30 years but could not remember being any busier than he had been the past few months. As executive pastor of the large First Baptist Church of Oak Forest, he had extensive responsibilities. The new pastor had arrived one year earlier and contacted John to consider joining the staff team. John felt a good connection with the pastor and sensed a strong call. As a result, he was willing to leave an even larger church to come to Oak Forest. John had not experienced any regrets about the move. The pace had been torrid, but the results had been satisfying. Now some well-deserved vacation time and rest were just the break he needed. Unfortunately, a phone call from a deacon would not only end the vacation but also present one of the most difficult challenges John had faced in his ministry.

Oak Forest was a medium-sized suburban city on the southern side of a metropolitan area of over one million. Until the last few years, it had consisted of an almost exclusively Anglo population that had grown steadily in the typical suburban flight pattern. The city was, for the most part, a conglomerate of subdivisions that were mainly a mix of middle- and upper-middle-income families. Whether they lived in newer homes or older homes, the residents had a reputation for having well-kept dwellings with immaculate yards. Oak Forest was a close-knit community. Support for the local schools, sports programs, and various community activities was extremely strong. Crime was almost nonexistent. Residents of Oak Forest often jokingly described themselves as a bigger version of the legendary Mayberry of Andy Griffith fame. This mind-set and the characteristics of the community would have a significant impact in the response of the membership to the greatest crisis in the history of FBC Oak Forest.

Although there were more than a dozen churches in Oak Forest, FBC was by far the largest and the dominant center of the community. Approximately one out of every three homes in Oak Forest had at least one person who was a member of or attended FBC. Through the years, the overwhelming majority of those who had served in any leadership capacity in the city were members of FBC. Likewise, 90 to 95 percent of the typical Sunday morning attendees of the church lived within the city limits. During its peak years of attendance, one study of the relationship between Oak Forest and the church showed that the membership profile of the congregation closely paralleled the demographic traits of the city. As one pastor had said, FBC was Oak Forest, and Oak Forest was FBC.

As the community had grown, the church had also grown. Over a period of nearly 33 years, the church had more than doubled in size under the leadership of two pastors. During this period, through numerous building projects, the congregation developed one of the best physical plants of any church in the metropolitan area. Moreover, the quality of programs and ministries of FBC was in some respects equal to that found in megachurches. The friendliness, facilities, and ministries made such a strong impression that the majority of those who visited more than once joined the church. With an impressive history and high hopes for the future, the church had welcomed the new pastor, Ronnie Vickers.

Ronnie had been a pastor for nearly three decades and had experienced great success at his previous churches. In addition to graduate theological degrees, he held the Ph.D. in counseling from a state university. Ronnie was a gifted communicator, counselor, and pastoral caregiver as well as a leader with great interpersonal skills. One of his colleagues described him as "the complete minister." He and his family seemed to be the perfect fit. The church and community immediately embraced them. Ronnie's wife, Dana, quickly became involved in ministry at the church and soon was as beloved as the wives of previous pastors had been. Ronnie began several new ministries the first year, including an evangelism program that proved very successful. The congregation marveled that the new pastor was exceptionally talented in so many areas. Optimism abounded at FBC until an unexpected announcement.

The expectation of having a normal Sunday evening service turned out to be anything but that. Ronnie preached as usual, but then came the stunning announcement. With no prior notice to the church leadership, Ronnie resigned as pastor effective immediately. The straightforward and unemotional manner in which he announced his resignation seemed bizarre. He gave little or no explanation. He had not even told his wife of his intentions until

> *He had not even told his wife of his intentions until that afternoon.*

that afternoon. He only related that God was leading him to leave FBC, and he was interested in pursuing some teaching opportunities. Predictably, the congregation was dumbfounded and shocked. No one could remember FBC having a pastor resign so suddenly and mysteriously. The trauma for the church was in some ways more intense than if a fire or a storm had destroyed the physical plant of which they were so proud.

The special status of the pastor in both the church and the community intensified the trauma of Ronnie's resignation. High esteem for the position of pastor at FBC was predominant in the community as well as the church. As the key image-maker for the church, his presence at community events was both expected and appreciated. Considering the strength of the church and what they considered an ideal community setting, the membership could not imagine that any minister would want to be anywhere else. Indeed, the church was generous and supportive of its pastor in many ways. The church anticipated no less than for their pastor to serve out his entire ministry and retire there.

Immediately after the resignation, there was rampant speculation about "the real reason" for the pastor's resignation. Even John, the executive pastor, had received no prior notice. When a deacon called him on his vacation, John was as mystified as the deacons were. After returning to Oak Forest and meeting with Ronnie, John uncovered no new information of substance. Ronnie simply said that God had led him to resign, and he was moving on to whatever opportunities God had for him. As he tried to make sense of the resignation, John thought that perhaps Ronnie was experiencing burnout. Many congregants concluded the same, and that explanation seemed logical for several reasons.

FBC was good to their pastors, but the pastoral duties were intense. The expectations of the congregation for preaching were very high, but they were quite challenging in other areas as well. Despite being a large church, whenever possible the members still liked the personal touch from the pastor for ministry needs. In addition, according to the church constitution, the pastor was the administrator. Even with the support of an excellent staff, these pressures appeared to provide a formula for burnout. Ronnie had met or exceeded these expectations, but had the stress been too much? Was Ronnie the victim of burnout?

John was in a difficult position. The deacon chairman had asked him to preach the Sunday following Ronnie's resignation. What would he preach? He felt led to bring a reassuring message. John recalled one key point of his message: "I'll support my pastor as he feels God's leading. . . . Needless to say, he was our pastor and he should do what God wants him to do, while the church moves on from here." John's message strengthened the resolve of the church to move forward. Immediately, another stabilizing force was the calling of a beloved former pastor to serve as interim. Despite his poor health, this pastor's presence and leadership brought a calming effect on the congregation.

Through the first few weeks, Ronnie remained resolute that God was leading him to do something else. He reaffirmed his desire to teach on the college level. For the first month, Ronnie took some time away from the church. When he and his family began attending again, the church had difficulty accepting that he was no longer the pastor. Like the church, Dana was struggling. She could not understand his abrupt resignation—it just did not make any sense. She loved being a pastor's wife and was grieving over the loss of that role. More importantly, she loved Ronnie. She was prepared to stand by her husband no matter what. Like others, Dana assumed Ronnie was experiencing burnout. Two months after the resignation, she would find out the devastating truth.

Ronnie had resigned because the seemingly ideal nature of his ministry was about to be shattered. Shortly before he resigned, Ronnie received a visit by someone from the church where he previously had been pastor. The news was cataclysmic for Ronnie. His moral failures at the church he served prior to coming to Oak Forest were about to come to the surface. Thus far, he had managed to keep his transgressions at his former church a secret. He somehow had unrealistically hoped it would continue that way. The pastor with an exemplary reputation who was held in such high esteem by the church membership was about to become badly tarnished. He did not wish to put the church through all that inevitably would ensue. To spare the church as much distress as possible, he resigned and sought to distance himself from the congregation.

> . . . the seemingly ideal nature of his ministry was about to be shattered.

After the leadership and the congregation learned the reason behind Ronnie's resignation, working through the consequences was a daunting task. A number of factors intensified the challenge. First, there was the confluence of emotions. A strong consensus existed that Ronnie had been an outstanding pastor in every way. The membership had especially embraced his preaching, which exceeded the high expectations of the church. This fact led to bewilderment. How was it possible to preach such great sermons while having failed to live up to those ideals? How could one have such inconsistencies? Some were ready to forgive, whereas others harbored deep resentment against the former pastor.

A second factor, which was particularly challenging, was the leadership structure that made the pastor the church administrator. No mechanism was in place for the staff to fill the administrative void. In the absence of a pastor, key deacons took charge of most of the important decisions. The church leadership affirmed and appreciated the staff, but they did not view them as having a major role in certain key leadership decisions. On some occasions, lay leaders asked staff members to leave meetings when discussion turned to these issues. Some staff members felt relieved not to have to bear the burden of the decisions, but others felt shunned. In any event, the staff was in the difficult position of being asked questions by the general membership and not having any answers. Naturally, some congregants thought the staff members were holding out on them.

A third factor that exacerbated the crisis was the circumstances of the community. Oak Forest had grown, in part, through suburban flight. Three types of people primarily made up the population of Oak Forest: long-time residents who had deep roots in the city for many years, persons who had moved from adjacent southside communities, and a lesser number of outsiders who had married in or moved in from somewhere outside the general southside metro area. For some of these residents, Oak Forest was a refuge from the demographic change that had been occurring on the southern side of the metropolitan area for over three decades. Yet, in the 10 years prior to Ronnie's coming, Oak Forest had begun to see a gradual change in its demographic makeup. Through a combination of annexation and transition, the city had gone from more than 98 percent Anglo to approximately 85 percent. The results were anything but negative. The total Anglo population remained stable. Property values increased, and crime was as low as ever. In addition, the county constructed a new elementary school in the city. The quality of life was superb. However, among some residents, a certain uneasiness began to develop that the community eventually would become like other surrounding areas. They feared the possibility of rising crime, declining schools, and falling property values. Nonetheless, most residents had no immediate plans to leave the life they had grown to love in Oak Forest.

In Oak Forest, the number one stabilizing element was the churches, the most influential of which was First Baptist Church. The church provided much of the glue that held the community together. However, the deep despair over the circumstances of the pastor's resignation combined in a perfect storm of unfortunate timing with the rising anxieties over racial transition and some local events in the schools. The county had begun to bus in a minority population from one of the high-crime areas of a nearby suburban city to attend Oak Forest High School. Predictably, tensions rose. Various incidents and rumors of gang activity unnerved parents. In addition, a failure to achieve a long-anticipated school redistricting brought further consternation. The redistricting would have annexed an adjacent community that was predominantly Anglo into the school zone for Oak Forest, and called for the building of a new middle school. With FBC in severe turmoil and concern growing in the community, the suburban flight that had brought so many to Oak Forest began to reverse. The Anglo population began to move out at a much faster rate. One prominent member later commented, "The community would not have accelerated its flight if Ronnie had stayed here. Many of them were staying here for the church, for the fellowship, and for the preaching. Therefore, when he did resign, they were shocked. . . . I have heard many people saying that if that had not happened, Oak Forest would not be where it is now, good or bad."

One noticeable change in the aftermath of Ronnie's resignation was the deterioration of the trust in pastoral leadership. Ronnie's successor came in as a well-known leader in Baptist circles. In the past, FBC would have had an immediate confidence in the new pastor. However, the new pastor found that leadership was much more challenging. He would have to overcome a cynicism that had emerged among some members. Unfortunately, this factor would hinder him the entire time he was the pastor there.

With the turmoil created by the resignation and the corresponding decline in the Anglo population, attendance at FBC began to plummet. Despite the best efforts of the new pastor and church leadership, the decline continued. Within five years, attendance was only slightly more than half of its peak. Many members who still lived in the community had become discouraged and stopped coming. Yet through this time of trial, a new outlook was emerging, and different ideas were beginning to ferment.

FBC had been open to other races attending services, but the almost exclusively white membership had not connected to the non-Anglo population. On multiple occasions, church members had gone door to door inviting all residents to visit the church, including those who lived in predominantly minority population subdivisions. Yet this approach failed to reach the rising non-Anglo population. However, the shrinking attendance had been a wake-up call for the church. Previously, the church could have had a predominantly Anglo membership and thrived. Members began to realize that demographic conditions were changing. If the congregation did not broaden its reach to the entire community, it would cease to know the vibrancy it had come to enjoy.

During the years following Ronnie's resignation, occasionally visitors from the various ethnic and racial groups that had moved to the community would attend FBC worship services. However, a much more substantial difference was the change in the constituency of the weekday education program. It became a virtual mirror of the changing demographics of the community. As a very large program, it always had been key in the growth of the church. It now became an even more critical factor in building bridges to the newer residents of the city. The younger couples who had chosen to stay rather than leave the community became particularly significant in developing a relationship to the non-Anglo population.

In addition to crossing barriers with increased intentionality, the congregation learned some new lessons about grace. Some were painful. These lessons started with forgiveness for the former pastor. Ronnie had divorced Dana, remarried, and moved to another city. Although Ronnie was no longer in vocational ministry, he was going through intensive Bible study as part of a personal restoration process. Six months after the new pastor came, Ronnie asked whether he could reconcile with the church through apologizing in person to either the deacons or the church. The new pastor and the executive pastor thought this would be a good way to help the church to heal. However, fearing a negative reaction, some key lay leaders tabled the idea. At the same time, a forgiving process toward the former pastor was occurring. Despite the moral failures, Ronnie still was loved. The members who did not move or become inactive tended to be more reconciling. After Ronnie's successor resigned several years later, one key leader remarked that if a full restoration had been possible, the overwhelming majority of the church would have taken Ronnie back as pastor.

In ministering to Dana, the congregation grew in understanding of the depth of God's healing and sustaining grace. Two months after she learned the truth about Ronnie's moral failures, he asked for the divorce. Dealing with the shock of Ronnie's resignation, the discovery of his immorality, and then the divorce brought a devastating sense of loss. She needed an anchor. With a teaching position at the local school and a desire to keep stability for her son, she had no plans to move. But could she continue to be a member of FBC? If she stayed there, how would the church receive her?

During the initial weeks after the divorce, Dana visited her parents' church a few times. However, she realized that FBC was her spiritual home. She needed the ministry of the church more than ever. They did not fail her. Some months later, Dana not only became active in the single adults ministry but also started a successful divorce recovery group. Dana dedicated herself to a study of the Scriptures concerning the issue of divorce and God's restorative grace. With this concertedly biblical approach and under Dana's leadership, the church began to experience a significant ministry to divorcees. One particularly powerful moving moment came during an Easter service when she took part in a skit. She initially showed one side of a placard with the word "divorced." As a testimony of God's wonderful grace, she then flipped the card to the other side to show "joy and contentment." The affirmation from the church was overwhelming. The church members realized the sufficiency of God's grace.

Despite signs of healing, some members were losing hope. With the steep decline of attendance and the closure of a number of predominantly Anglo churches on the southside, the ultimate disbanding of the church seemed unavoidable to some. In the background, a few members were calling for the church to prepare for its inevitable closing. However, many more members were determined that the church would not die. One key indicator of their resoluteness was that the church finances remained strong. Even during the five-year decline following Ronnie's resignation, the church was able to pay off all but a small portion of a $3.3 million debt.

When a new pastor followed Ronnie Vickers's successor, the church had been through a gradual process of healing, which in part was the result of good leadership from the interim pastor. Under the visionary leadership of the new pastor, attendance began to rise significantly. In the first few months, an influx of new members equaled the rate of previous high-growth periods in the church's history. The church was reaching people with some fresh ideas of connecting to the community, including a massive effort during the Christmas season with a reproduction of the biblical village of Bethlehem. The participation of the church membership in producing this event and the large number of visitors who came indicated the renewal of the church and its relationship to the community. Morale was beginning to return to the level of the peak attendance years. Within less than a year of the new pastor's arrival, the debt was completely retired. The church celebrated this accomplishment as more evidence that the future for FBC Oak Forest was bright.

Beyond the Story: Leadership Lessons

The Unique Consequences of Moral Failure

Moral failure is a different kind of crisis from others. One unique aspect concerns the severe nature of the disillusionment and anger and the varied ways people respond to the crisis. Church members often manifest sharp differences of opinion about how the congregation should handle the fallout. Even if division does not exist prior to the moral failure of a ministry leader, it likely will afterward. Another unique aspect of moral failure is the manner in which it may bring forth negative

> *Moral failure is a different kind of crisis from others.*

consequences from preexisting vulnerabilities. While all crises tend to expose weak points of a church or ministry, moral failure does so more intensely. At FBC, the crisis with the pastor interacted with the growing gap between the community and the church demographics to create the perfect storm of trial. Yet in such cases, a church may have challenges even with a characteristic that appears to be positive. In this instance, the high esteem that the congregation afforded the pastor meant that the impact of his fall was even more devastating. Additionally, more so than other crises, moral failures require an extended time of healing. Church members do not easily work through the emotions and consequences that result. FBC Oak Forest experienced these uniquely difficult and catastrophic consequences of moral failure.

Key Factors in the Crisis and the Recovery

An examination of the crisis event at FBC and its outcomes revealed several significant factors. First, the resignation of Ronnie was a reminder that a healthy church should not become overly dependent on the pastor's leadership in the key administrative functions of the church. If a shared leadership role had been in place, the transition would have been less difficult. Churches that employ a team concept of leadership and develop leaders at every level are in a stronger position to cope with acute crises as well as normative leadership challenges.

Second, the growing dissonance between FBC and its community intensified the crisis. The church affirmed that biblically, they needed to reach everyone in the surrounding area, and anyone who came to FBC received a warm welcome. Indeed, FBC was more welcoming of non-Anglos than many of the other churches in the southside area. However, the church had not developed an intentional strategy to reach a changing demographic composition. The numerous strengths of FBC had masked this weakness. The pastor's fall revealed the weakness in glaring fashion. Perhaps unintentionally, FBC was relying on a homogeneous demographic that no longer existed in Oak Forest. Such has been the case in many communities where Southern Baptists have been the dominant denominational identity. The homogeneous strategy has ceased to be a successful model for Southern Baptists in an ever-diversifying twenty-first-century American demographic.

Third, as with many churches, FBC had little structure to deal with a large-scale falling away. Members who became discouraged and stopped attending worsened the pain of losing those who left the church or the community. The decline had a cascading effect of negative influence.

FBC lacked an effective means to consistently contact and care for the members who were becoming inactive or in danger of leaving altogether. A church with a healthy system of caring for and staying in touch with its members has a safety net when the crises come. Without this comprehensive safety net, attendance at FBC plummeted.

Fourth, while the five years for Ronnie's successor as pastor was a tough time for him and the church, it set the stage for a resurgence. While it would be a misnomer to consider him a sacrificial lamb, the church needed time to resolve the issues of its shattered confidence in its pastor and a rapidly changing community. A season for grieving and reassessment was a necessary foundation for recovery. Churches that have experienced the moral failure of a leader must be intentional in providing adequate time for healing before attempting to move forward in new directions.

Fifth, while some members were leaving or becoming inactive, the committed core refused to quit. Following a crisis, enlarging the core and developing its spiritual depth should be a priority. If the size of the committed core is too small in comparison with the size of the membership and other regular attendees, the church will be extremely vulnerable during crises. At FBC, the committed core was large enough to keep the church alive until the situation improved. This commitment was particularly evident in the financial support that greatly reduced the debt even while the attendance was falling rapidly.

Visionary leadership is the most effective type of leadership for a turnaround situation.

Finally, visionary leadership was essential to the recovery of the church. After Ronnie left, the pastor search committee reflected a conviction among the church leadership that God still had great things in store for FBC. As a result, the committee did not look for a pastor to be a caretaker to a declining church. Because they had a vision, they searched for a visionary pastor who believed in a positive future for the congregation. When the new pastor came, a renewed momentum reclaimed some members who had been on the sidelinescarried the church through the tough times felt reenergized. Together the church moved forward again. Visionary leadership is the most effective type of leadership for a turnaround situation. At FBC, it proved to be the most critical component in recovering from a moral catastrophic crisis.

Questions for Further Thought

1. What would have been some of the potential benefits as well as problems if the leadership had allowed the former pastor to come back and apologize for his moral failure? Should the pastor and associate pastor have insisted that the church allow the former pastor to come back and apologize? If allowed to come, should he have appeared before the entire church or just the deacons? Would it make a difference if a fallen leader other than the former pastor wanted to make an apology before the church?

2. In view of the expectations of some members, should staff members have protested their exclusion from the process of making certain key decisions?

3. Why do church leaders often not face a changing community context until it becomes a crisis? How can you identify the attitudes and roadblocks prior to a community change?

4. What steps should a new leader take to deal with the loss of trust because of failures of a predecessor?

5. How can a more diversified leadership base insulate a church from the potential damage of a catastrophic crisis?

6. What role does giving the church time to heal have in preparing for resurgence? What positive actions should the leadership take in this season in the life of a church?

7. How did the loss of trust in the office of pastor affect the loss of the church's vision?

8. How can visionary leadership work in a church that has suffered significant loss? How must the visionary leader be sensitive to the context?

9. What are some safeguards that leaders and churches can establish to help deter moral failure?

First Baptist Church, Lindale. PHOTO BY JAMES F. COOK.

Chapter 7

When the Dream Is Shattered

"'No weapon formed against you will succeed, and you will refute any accusation raised against you in court. This is the heritage of the LORD's servants, and their righteousness is from Me.' This is the LORD's declaration." Isaiah 54:17

First Baptist Church, Lindale

Lindale is an old mill town with a population of a little over 4,000 located in Floyd County in northwestern Georgia. At its peak, the mill employed over 2,000 people, and Lindale was overflowing with large, working-class families. With the mills long closed, Lindale has transitioned to being a bedroom community for the adjacent, medium-sized city of Rome, Georgia. Lindale's mostly Anglo (95 percent) population is mainly middle-class and lower-middle-class families.

First Baptist Church Lindale began in 1898 and has had a long history closely connected with the town. In 1981, during the height of mill employment, the mill company donated a recreation center to the church, which is still in use by the church. With the decline of the mills and resultant job losses, FBC Lindale had a significant drop in attendance. For nearly 20 years, the church was unable to regain its previous attendance highs. However, when Pastor Tim Burnham arrived in 1992, the church began to see significant growth. Attendance more than doubled over the next 13 years, with Sunday school attendance well over 450 and worship attendance of more than 550.

The new vibrancy of FBC Lindale was evident not only in attendance but also in evangelism. The year before Tim became the pastor, the church recorded only eight baptisms. The development of a witness-training program and the evangelistic preaching of the pastor were keys to the turnaround. In 2003, the church baptized a record 108. The congregation went from being one of the least effective churches in terms of ratio of baptisms to membership to being consistently one of the top churches in the Floyd County Association as well as the Georgia Baptist Convention. The congregation had three morning services, but they were not enough. FBC Lindale was out of room.

Tim considered the space issue a serious challenge. The church had become regional in its ministry. Although its predominant base remained the town of Lindale, people were driving from various areas of Floyd County to be a part of this dynamic, growing church. With 70 percent of Floyd County unchurched, Tim could not rest with the church not being able to grow further. For him, reaching the community was of eternal importance. He also knew that if the church did not move forward, it inevitably would stagnate and decline.

The challenges of having a building program at the current site were overwhelming. The church was landlocked, bordered by a river and a train track. Trains frequently came by during the Sunday morning services. The loud noise, to which the congregation had grown accustomed, was a challenge for guest speakers. Upon beginning his message, one visiting preacher joked that he had heard that the church would tolerate a one-train interrupted sermon, but they would become restless if the preacher spoke long enough to have two trains interrupt him. However, the deacons would come forward and close the service if the sermon was long enough that three trains passed! When coincidentally a second train passed just as he was finishing his message, the congregation broke into laughter.

The church faced a more serious challenge than the train track. Ninety percent of the 12 acres the church occupied was on a flood plain. In some places, the property was as much as eight feet below the flood plain. Only one piece of land near the church was available for purchase. Being across the street, it would have offered little relief. In addition, the owner was asking over six times its appraised value.

Tim was not sure what the answer would be, but he was confident that God would provide a way for the church to continue to grow. He put together a vision team of 18 people, whom he chose deliberately to represent the various ministries and age groups of the church. In addition, the team represented a balance in terms of long-time members and relatively new members. Most importantly, the congregation highly respected the members of the vision team for their spiritual commitment and leadership influence. The group seemed ideal to carry out the task of leading the congregation toward fulfilling God's purpose for FBC Lindale.

While the committee was carefully weighing the limited options, Tim studied the concept of multiple church campuses. He realized that a church like FBC Lindale would not likely be willing to abandon its historical ties to the current property. Why should they not consider being one church with two locations? The church had no debt. If they could find a nearby place to meet that could attract as many as 200 current attendees plus new visitors, both locations could grow at the same time. Tim hoped the traditionalists who wanted nothing to change at the current location would be pleased. Congregants of a more adventurous spirit would have an exciting new place to worship and even more reason to invite their lost friends. The option seemed to be a win-win for everyone. The committee embraced the idea with unanimity and great excitement. They brought their recommendation to the deacons, who received it positively with no dissent.

With the main leadership seemingly on board, the next step was a church-wide meeting. Interest was high, and members packed the auditorium for the presentation. "I shared the vision with them, not my personal agenda but as a kingdom vision. I spoke about one church with two locations, the benefits, rewards and the fact that we could see a lot of people saved," Tim recalled. From every indication the pastor and vision committee could discern, the reaction of the members to the presentation was extremely positive. The committee members even received letters commending them for their work. Yet the committee took nothing for granted. They scheduled a number of additional meetings with various ministries and groups within the church to explain the plan carefully. The vision committee addressed potential concerns such as: Would the present property be mortgaged or sold? Would the present location ever be abandoned? Would the church become divided? The answers of the committee appeared to resolve any lingering doubt. As a result, the agenda went forward with a set date to vote on the move. The initial vote would be strictly on the concept. The church was not committing to any specific action other than to adopt the plan.

As the church moved toward the vote, there were no overt objections. However, small signs began to appear that there was opposition to the plan. Rumors started swirling that "some people are not happy," but nothing came to the surface. Then the first bombshell hit when someone mailed an anonymous letter to the entire congregation. The target was the minister of music and his style of music as well as some of the staff. Much of it did not relate directly to the proposed concept of one church at two locations. However, the resultant negativism dampened the enthusiasm for the idea. When the vote came, the results were disappointing. Only 71 percent voted for having one church at two locations. Undaunted, the vision team and deacons were convinced that there were simply some misunderstandings. They held more meetings in the belief that additional communication would alleviate any fears that some might have. Discussions were for the most part very positive, and the leadership pressed forward.

> *Then the first bombshell hit when someone mailed an anonymous letter to the entire congregation.*

Unfortunately, as plans moved forward so did the anonymous letter campaign. Someone or some group sent the first of seven additional letters to the congregation. These letters had an especially vicious tone. The letters attacked the congregation and its leadership. Each letter was more venomous than the previous. One letter declared, "For those who think dividing our church, splitting our fellowship, and causing conflicts with God's people is the thing they need to do, we should accept their resignations, bid them God's Speed, and continue our work here. Let them go. But leave our people alone." The letters were obviously disturbing, and church members wanted to know their source. Although keeping a secret in a small-town Baptist church is difficult, no one was talking. The vision team and deacons did not know the source of the letters.

> *Although keeping a secret in a small-town Baptist church is difficult, no one was talking.*

Although the church leaders would not discover the full picture until later, someone had targeted FBC Lindale as part of a larger attack on six Baptist churches in the Floyd County Association. The attacks stemmed from one church that adopted a contemporary model of worship along with some innovative methods of outreach. The new efforts paid off as the formerly stagnant church began to grow. Sadly, some of the long-term members were in fierce opposition. One man in particular, a deacon, would make this campaign a personal vendetta. He lashed out against not only his own church leadership but also other Baptist churches in the area that had seen significant growth, particularly if they utilized innovative means. FBC Lindale, because it was considering the concept of two locations, was a natural target.

Clandestinely, the deacon began to build a network of a few disgruntled people in the six churches. Being prominent in the community, he began to write caustically critical editorials about "new methods" in area churches. The local paper published these editorials. The focal point of the editorial venom was that these churches were following the Purpose-Driven Church model of ministry advocated by Rick Warren. By no means had these churches simply adopted Warren's methods wholesale. Nonetheless, objection to this paradigm provided a rallying point. Later, FBC Lindale leaders discovered that the agenda of the group was nothing less than to see the pastors of the six churches "leave Floyd County."

The writer of the editorials had developed a movement that was gaining momentum, although it remained mostly hidden. If anyone outside the group knew that more was going on than just the editorials, they were keeping quiet.

Back at FBC Lindale, the pastor and other leaders had yet to make a connection between the editorials and the undercurrent they were experiencing, but the connection was real. The anonymous letters kept coming, and all efforts to determine who was writing them were to no avail. When one of the letters said that the vision team and deacons were not in total agreement, Tim knew that he and the church leadership had to meet the dissension head on. He called a special deacons meeting and asked every deacon four questions: (1) "Do you support the direction of the church?" (2) "Do you support the pastor?" (3) "Did you write the letters?" (4) "Did you know who was writing the letters?" With the exception of one deacon, all the deacons answered affirmatively to the first two questions and no to the last two questions. The lone deacon had previously stated that he was in favor of the vision team's recommendation, but in actuality he had been in league with the editorial writer from the other church. He apparently had been distributing various materials that not only were very much against the Purpose-Driven Church model but also contained a number of false accusations. He had conspired with an inactive deacon at FBC Lindale and some others in undermining the vision team's effort. In the meeting, the pastor and the rest of the deacon body boldly confronted him concerning his duplicity. The dissident deacon resigned the next day.

Now that the opposition was somewhat out in the open, the vision committee and deacons hoped they could deal with the issues in a positive fashion. The next scheduled vote would be for the actual implementation of the project. They had a reason for their optimism. As the committee continued to work, a wonderful option developed. A church building for sale by another denomination, perfectly suited for a second location for FBC Lindale, had become available at a bargain price. Located off a major thoroughfare and with great visibility, it had obvious potential as a place that could facilitate rapid growth in attendance. In addition, it was only five miles from the current church site. The location was close enough to allow the pastor to travel quickly back and forth for multiple services. It was also in close proximity to the homes of many of the current members. The committee was convinced that God had answered their prayers. How could anyone oppose what was obviously a divine provision?

Unfortunately, emotion was already taking prominence over logic and spiritual discernment. At a church conference meeting prior to the Sunday morning vote, the formal motion and discussion of the proposal were on the agenda. In anticipation of fireworks, the church leadership secured an outside moderator. At the beginning of the meeting, the congregation adopted a motion to adhere to time limits and require members to speak to the issues rather than conduct personal attacks. Although some amendments to the proposal were defiantly offered, they were each defeated handily. However, opponents of the recommendation had been hard at work capitalizing on the fears of long-time and fringe members. Their efforts were casting a shadow over the upcoming Sunday vote. The division in the congregation was increasing.

> *In anticipation of fireworks, the church leadership secured an outside moderator.*

Still hopeful, the pastor, staff, and leadership were dismayed when the Sunday morning vote showed only 60 percent supported the implementation. The tactic of the opposition was to mobilize every possible negative vote. People who had not been to the church in years came to vote against the plans. One man who was a self-proclaimed atheist, but whose name was still on the roll, came and voted. However, most surprising was the conspicuous absence of many who had professed support, even strong support. The number who voted for the implementation was far less than the vote for the concept. The opposition actually had eight fewer votes, but there were also 117 fewer positive votes. The reason for the absence of the professed supporters became all too apparent. They simply did not want to be involved in controversy. They had been intimidated into not expressing their convictions. If they had come and voted, the positive percentage would have been significantly higher.

Of all the stress that Tim had been through, the absence of these supporters was particularly discouraging. As he thought over who had not come, he felt personal hurt. Many of them were people for whom he had gone a second ministry mile. Had not the countless hours of pastoral care at least yielded enough appreciation that they would come and support their pastor and leadership in a cause for which they had professed support? Their absence was both mysterious and devastatingly disappointing.

For Tim it seemed that the church had experienced a catastrophic crisis of leadership. The approach of the leaders could have served as a textbook example of how to do the vision process. They utilized the best possible cross-section of members. The pastor had an especially high credibility for his 13 years of dedicated service, which had yielded the greatest growth the church had ever experienced. The leadership had painstakingly communicated their ideas to the congregation. The leaders had also listened to concerns and given thoughtful answers. Most important, a provision that they felt certain was from God and that exceeded even their best hopes had become available. What had gone wrong? A small group from both within and without the church had sowed discord in the congregation. Those who would stop at nothing less than seeing the pastor and staff leave FBC Lindale had gained a foothold.

> *For Tim it seemed that the church had experienced a catastrophic crisis of leadership.*

Tim quickly realized that he could not afford to be melancholy. Despite the vote and the tactics of the opposition, the pastor, the vision committee, and the deacons discerned that the overwhelming majority of the active church was in favor of the vision team's recommendation. They estimated that the real hard-core opposition was no more than 50 people and maybe as few as 25. This number represented only between 5 and 10 percent of the Sunday morning attendance. They would not give up hope but would proceed cautiously, depending on God to lead them.

What would the next step be? They would not have to wait long for a stunning turn of events.

Pending the outcome of the vote, the church had not yet signed a contract to purchase the building. In good faith they had negotiated with the church that wanted to sell the facility. At no time had the seller given any indication that there was another buyer. The day after the vote, the news came that an unnamed buyer had signed a contract through an attorney that would tie up the property for six months to allow for survey work. The timing seemed suspicious. The church leadership never learned who tied up the property, but Tim had always preached that God was in ultimate control. The congregation would have their faith tested.

With the option closed and a divided congregation, the pastor and leadership knew they had a major task before them. They went to work at damage control. First, there was the issue of congregational morale. The impact of the caustic criticism of the staff and deacons had shocked the church. They wondered how anyone could act that way. "We were embarrassed and had to answer a lot of questions in the community and even in the grocery stores. People used to say good things about the church, but now they had only bad things to say about it. That was demoralizing to our members," Tim remembered. "After the vote, the church thought they had gone through the battle, and they were willing to run up the hill behind the flag. But what devastated them was the turn of events. They thought they had done everything right and won, yet God himself had shut that door. This stunned everybody the morning after," Tim recalled.

To meet the morale challenge, Tim preached positive biblical messages. His first series, from Nehemiah, focused on encouragement and having an optimistic vision. He asked the music minister to concentrate on uplifting music that focused on praising God in worship. When Tim finished the Nehemiah series, he pulled from his files some of the strongest sermons he had preached during his time at Lindale. The congregation responded positively to the tone of the worship and the content of the sermons. The pastor's wife, Charlene, also tried to promote a positive climate. "I believe I was the first one who stood out of the rubble and . . . [did] something normal by organizing a women's holiday brunch, because we had been doing abnormal things for a long time," she remembered.

Although slow at first, the situation began to turn for the better. Little by little, the congregation was regaining its pre-crisis atmosphere.

During the recovery period, a second challenge was dealing with the ill feelings between the two sides. Again, the response was biblical. The pastor and leadership were determined to set the example and be gracious no matter how caustic the criticism would become. It was not easy. It was hard not to harbor anger at the hateful actions. As Tim expressed, "I could have buried the people that we had to confront, but I was very gracious to them." Some of the leaders struggled to control their tempers. On a number of occasions, the pastor had to be the soothing voice to keep the leadership from returning fire, especially during business meetings. Tim found that trying to keep the peace was physically, emotionally, and spiritually draining. His wife later said the strain took a toll on his health.

> *On a number of occasions, the pastor had to be the soothing voice to keep the leadership from returning fire. . . .*

Being kind and gracious in response to the ongoing attacks did not mean that church leaders could avoid tough confrontations. It was biblical for the pastor and leaders to deal with those creating the divisiveness. In addition, the church constitution called for all the members to come together in unity and harmony once the majority had spoken on a particular matter. A member might not agree with a decision. However, FBC Lindale expected all members to support the outcome of the vote and not create further divisiveness over the issue.

Much of the opposition was still beneath the surface. In order to bring resolution, the leadership needed to expose and confront it. Yet how could they identify the opposition, whose tactics had been deliberately clandestine? An opportunity presented itself through the text of one of the anonymous letters, which called for the members of FBC Lindale to withhold their tithes and offerings in protest of the potential move and the leadership. To stop the further spread of division, the church refused to allow members who were withholding their giving to serve in leadership. The nominating committee was careful to ask all the candidates for positions in the church for the coming year whether they were in support of the leadership. As a result, some of the dissidents left.

A watershed moment came when the pastor and leaders discovered that the strife at FBC Lindale had been part of a larger movement. The pastor brought the whole situation to light at the end of his Sunday morning sermon. He shared that the relocation issue had been merely a vehicle for a larger agenda: to remove him and five other pastors. The overwhelming majority of the congregation was astounded and angry, whereas members who had been involved did not deny it. Tim recalled, "That was a huge turning point as the whole congregation, including the deacons, came together to stand by me and the staff. And that was when the group saw that they had lost the battle."

Many months of healing would remain. Virtually all the opposition group eventually left. Unfortunately, because of the setback, some of the strong visionary leadership left as well. The conflict had worn them out, and they did not have the desire to try to rebuild. Remarkably, in experiencing a crisis that would have destroyed the fellowship of many churches beyond repair, FBC Lindale remained stable. Attendance dropped 14 percent, and offerings declined accordingly. Yet the pastor and leadership were grateful to God for seeing them through. It could have been much worse. Having gone through the crisis, they were convinced that God would provide them with a new plan, one that would enable them to reach Lindale and the surrounding area for Christ in a greater way than before.

Beyond the Story: Leadership Lessons

Key Factors for Minimizing the Fallout and Reviving the Vision

Several factors helped FBC Lindale not only to minimize the negative fallout of the crisis but eventually to find healing and a recovery of its vision. Of course, not all the factors were equal in terms of the level of proficiency with which the leadership applied them. Nonetheless, each was crucial in allowing FBC Lindale to reemerge with a hopeful future.

First, Tim had given the congregation a strong foundation of biblical preaching. More than 13 years of expository preaching had given a framework for the church to stay focused on biblical priorities. Strategic preaching—that is, preaching that leads the church to understand what it means to be the people of God—was critically important. The focus on the book of Nehemiah provided a biblical perspective of how to process the difficult events that occurred. When the opportunity to buy the property was lost, this biblical viewpoint enabled the congregation to avoid a blaming mode. Instead, they believed that for some unknown reason God had allowed this door to close. As a result, they also believed God would open another door.

Second, the long tenure of the pastor had established a trust that kept the core of the church together. With only one or two exceptions, neither the deacon body nor the 18-member vision team wavered during the entire crisis. Early in the pastor's ministry, this might not have been the case. FBC Lindale had faced some difficult problems during the time of Tim's ministry. On more than one occasion, some members had seriously challenged Tim's leadership. Five years earlier a small group had tried to force him to leave. Their efforts did not get very far. Yet working through these difficulties brought a higher level of respect for the pastor. The overwhelming majority of the church had seen their pastor stand tall in the midst of testing and trial. They knew he would not falter under pressure.

The long tenure had given time for the development of solid leadership. The strong evangelism program that had been in place for nearly eight years had produced a large number of church members who knew how to share their faith. Scripture memorization and an emphasis on a vibrant testimony, both a part of the evangelism program, were significant factors in developing the spiritual maturity of the participants. Likewise, ongoing men's ministries and women's ministries, a strong Sunday school, and other discipleship programs had deepened the spiritual life of the church. Many of these members who had grown spiritually in the last 13 years were now serving in key areas of the church.

A third factor in managing the crisis was the determined effort to communicate. Counteracting the clandestine campaign of secret meetings and anonymous letters was a difficult challenge. The main issue was the element of surprise. The church leadership was unprepared for how many votes the opposition secured and the number of potential positive votes that were neutralized. Apparently, the feedback loop was not as strong as it should have been. A significant number of members were hiding their true feelings. Yet the numerous meetings that church leaders held with various groups in the congregation served the purpose of containing the damage. The meetings did not always draw the opposition into the daylight. However, they did present the facts that allowed most members to recognize the disinformation campaign for what it was. Particularly critical was the communication by the pastor at the end of the sermon when he revealed the true scope of the opposition. The core opposition group that was present that day could not deny that what the pastor was saying was true.

A fourth factor was the healthy way in which the pastor and leadership dealt with the opposition. In such cases, the default action is often conflict avoidance. Such was not the case at FBC Lindale. Instead, they combined firmness with kindness. During this time, the pastor worked continually to make sure no one in the congregation treated the opposition disrespectfully. The "confrontation in love" approach prevented the opposition from exerting increased influence from positions of leadership, and at the same time it minimized personal attacks and the resulting detrimental effects. An important aspect was to continue to minister to everyone regardless of the position they had taken. The pastor went the extra mile to minister to the opposition, particularly when they experienced crises of any kind. As a result, eventually even some who caused the most difficulty apologized and came back.

A fifth factor was a participatory leadership model. One of the charges leveled by the opposition was that "the pastor was running the church like a CEO." While the pastor and deacons did not believe this charge had any legitimacy, nonetheless, during the crisis it was especially important to exercise an inclusive style. In a crisis period, decisions cannot always wait on a committee meeting. Yet the authoritative style that is sometimes necessary and more accepted after a natural disaster would not have worked well in this case. Tim resisted the temptation to make hasty decisions and, as much as possible, worked through a process with the leadership structures in the church.

The inclusive style of leadership by Tim and key church leaders prevented the schism from becoming greater and accelerated the healing process. Unfortunately, their efforts were not completely successful. Apparently, they were unable to bring some opinion leaders into the process. Otherwise, the outside forces would not have been able to exert the negative influence that they did. It is possible that residue from the previous conflicts that Tim had faced a few years earlier was fertile ground for causing discontent. If so, it is a reminder that there must be a continual diligence to make certain that old conflicts do not reappear in new forms.

Moving Forward Again

Three and a half years after the initial concept vote, FBC Lindale once again was unified and reaching people. Tim noted that the prevailing thought had been that "we would lose half of our people." Yet the attendance was at 90 percent of what it was before the conflict. The church leadership was reconsidering ways to solve the limitations of the church facilities. The church not only survived but was healthy again.

> *It was quite a different outcome for Tim and FBC Lindale than some had plotted earlier.*

Weathering the crisis furthered the respect of the congregation for Tim's leadership. As an appreciation for Tim's 17 years of ministry at FBC Lindale, the church voted to give him a five-week sabbatical and $10,000 to use for a trip of a lifetime. The membership heartily and unanimously adopted the recommendation. It was quite a different outcome for Tim and FBC Lindale than some had plotted earlier.

Questions for Further Thought

1. In what ways would you attempt to respond to an anonymous letter campaign?

2. Why do you think the size of the initial negative vote surprised Tim and the leadership? What strategies might have improved the accuracy of the feedback?

3. When the first vote was not as strong, should Tim and the leadership have considered different options? If so, what would some of those options have been?

4. What could have been some reasons that so many who said they supported the vision team failed to come and vote? Why did the negative group gain momentum? What actions, if any, could have changed that?

5. What measures, if any, could have prevented some of the more progressive members from leaving after the two-campus opportunity fell through?

6. What would have been the pros and cons of Tim addressing the issues from the pulpit earlier than he did?

7. What role did the integrity of the leadership play in the eventual healing of this congregation? What lessons from this case study about the establishment of trust are applicable to other ministry settings?

8. Had Tim decided to move on during this battle, what could have been the result for him, the church, and the other churches in the area? If you were in his situation, and an attractive offer came from another church, would you be likely to accept it?

Frank and Debbie Cox at Pleasant Hill Baptist Church.
PHOTO USED BY PERMISSION FROM FRANK COX. FROM *TRUSTING GOD'S HEART: FINDING PEACE IN TIMES OF SORROW,* BAXTER PRESS, 2000.

Chapter 8

Crisis in the Midst of Crisis

"So the Lord blessed the last part of Job's life more than the first."   Job 42:12a

Frank Cox

Frank Cox and his wife, Debbie, knew in their hearts that Pleasant Hill Baptist Church in Duluth, Georgia, was the right place for them. Frank was about to graduate from New Orleans Baptist Theological Seminary. They had felt God was leading them to go back home to serve in the Atlanta area, and a friend had recommended Frank to the pastor search committee. The committee was very impressed that one of the references, Dr. Landrum Leavell, then president of New Orleans Baptist Theological Seminary, had given Frank such a high recommendation. Dr. Leavell noted that if Frank "could grow a church based on southeast Louisiana values, he could grow a church anywhere." Indeed, Frank came to Pleasant Hill Baptist Church with a phenomenal growth experience at the Barataria Baptist Church in Lafitte, Louisiana. In this very non-Baptist area at a small, struggling church that had seen little growth,

Frank led the church to a new evangelistic fervor with over 90 baptisms in less than three years.

Pleasant Hill Baptist Church needed a pastor who could lead it to grow. It was a church in decline, having lost 34 more members the previous year than had been added. The effect of Frank's ministry was immediate. The first year the church added 125 members, and the congregation was excited that they no longer were a dying church. The second year another 125 members were added, but toward the end of that year a negative reaction began to occur. Reflecting back, Frank realized that he should not have been surprised. Even in the process of his acceptance of the call, some clues indicated that the church was not healthy. Frank received an initial figure for the compensation package. Later, the offer was $4,000 less. Frank accepted the call but found out that not all members of the pastor search committee were aware of what had happened regarding the compensation passage. It was a sign of things to come.

The initial trouble at Pleasant Hill Baptist Church had centered on the election of leadership. As Frank recalled, "They had a game they would play with me, but they failed to tell me about all the rules of the game." In this game, the pastor would ask members who had served in leadership to pray about returning to their present places of service. Then they would return to him and say they had prayed and felt "it was not God's will for them to accept the position." According to Frank, those former leaders had expected him to beg and plead for them to take the position, to which they would respond by finally relenting and accepting the place of service. Instead, Frank took them at their word and moved on to more willing members of the church. As a result, at the end of the first two years the leadership structure had changed significantly. Along with the massive influx of new members, this new group of leaders made the old guard uncomfortable.

Gradually an opposition group began to form from those who previously had been in positions of leadership. But what could they say? The new pastor had led the church to unprecedented growth. Salvations were occurring at a much greater rate than the church had experienced before. The financial base had increased, and Frank was diligent in his pastoral care. Nonetheless, the criticism began to mount. Opponents distorted minor issues and made critical comments at business meetings. However, no apparent opportunities existed for the disgruntled to seize upon.

The constant criticism frustrated Frank. He began to consider whether the time had come for him to leave. He was well known and respected among many for his reputation as a growth pastor. Various search committees were interested and began to contact his references. Dr. Leavell, who once again was among Frank's references, began to get so many contacts that at an SBC convention he asked Frank what was happening. Sensing Frank's discouragement, Dr. Leavell advised him to stay put and "not to run when the heat was up" because he would likely end up "with the same type of church." Dr. Leavell's advice was particularly helpful with one very tempting offer. When Frank was finishing his Master of Divinity degree program, Dr. Joe Cothen, vice president for academic affairs at New Orleans Baptist Theological Seminary, had wanted Frank to stay to work on his Doctor of Theology degree in preaching. Now as the result of a recommendation from Dr. Cothen, a seemingly ideal situation was opening up. A strong church in the New Orleans area was very interested in Frank becoming their pastor. The congregation was more than willing to allow Frank to pursue his doctoral degree. Frank and Debbie visited the church in view of a call. As Frank listened carefully to the leadership, he realized that he would face some of the same problems at New Orleans that he was facing at Pleasant Hill. The advice of Dr. Leavell had been timely. Frank saw the experience as a reconfirmation that he was in God's will despite the growing opposition he was enduring.

> *He had taken the church van to the local hospital, parked it there, and then caught a bus to California.*

In the middle of Frank's fourth year, his critics finally had the opportunity they had been seeking. In a bizarre set of circumstances, unexpectedly and without any explanation, a ministerial staff member was gone for 10 days. He had taken the church van to the local hospital, parked it there, and then caught a bus to California. Such strange behavior was indicative of some serious issues with this staff member. As a result, Frank, the deacons, and the personnel committee decided that termination was necessary. However, at the last minute they hesitated to go through with it and "made a decision based on bad judgment," said Frank. They allowed him to come back for six months with the stipulation that they review the situation in three months. After the three months, it was apparent that giving him additional time had been a mistake. Frank, the deacons, and the personnel committee moved forward with termination. However, the result became a nightmare. The opponents of the pastor saw the staff issue as a chance to voice their objections to the new direction the church was taking. In an emotional business meeting, in which the opposition actually booed the leadership making the recommendation, the vote was 60 percent to 40 percent to allow the staff member to stay. The dissent was a serious crisis for Frank's ministry at Pleasant Hill Baptist Church, but he could not have imagined that a far worse trial was about to begin.

Two weeks after the business meeting, Frank was preaching the Easter service when he realized that his wife was not in her usual spot in the choir. Debbie was absent because she was experiencing some severe pain. Her left foot was incapacitated to the point that she could not keep her shoe on. Debbie had been enduring numbness on her left side for some time and had experienced a seizure during pregnancy. Yet medical examinations had yielded no explanation. The day after Easter, Frank knew that something was different. As they were eating in a restaurant, Debbie began having seizures. An immediate visit to the family doctor resulted in a referral to a neurologist, who quickly arranged some tests. The words from the neurologist were devastating: "Debbie, we have a major problem. The CT scan reveals that you have a malignant brain tumor, and the prognosis doesn't look good."[1]

The prognosis was so dire that the neurologist wanted to hospitalize Debbie that night. However, he relented when Frank and Debbie explained that they needed to make arrangements for the care of their two-year-old son, Stephen. On the way home from the doctor, the radio was playing the song with the words, "There is no mountain He cannot climb, no problem that He cannot solve." Frank and Debbie sang along with the words that would give them the strength they would need so much. Frank recalled, "When we got home, we saw that everything about our lives had changed, and there was nothing in our lives that was not touched by what had befallen us. When I came to church, I felt that I was in the presence of Satan, and when I came back home I saw that everything had changed." It was an overwhelming crisis in the midst of crisis. Frank later described it as "two black clouds" to deal with at the same time. In the coming days, both seemed to be getting darker.

Two days after the diagnosis, Debbie was in surgery. Looking out the window of the hospital, Frank asked, "God, where are You in all of this? I could take the problem at the church, but my wife?" But even the problems at the church had worsened. Within a few weeks after Debbie's surgery, Frank discovered

> ". . . God, where are You in all of this?"

new information about the staff member that was extremely serious. Deciding on a different tactic, Frank asked 10 inactive deacons to meet with the 15 active deacons. This strategy posed a dangerous risk. These inactive deacons were the core group for the opposition to Frank's ministry. However, having failed to terminate the staff member previously, Frank felt a unified front was the only way to deal with the situation with any hope of a resolution. When the inactive deacons saw the evidence, they immediately reversed their position and agreed to seek the termination of the staff member. With his support gone, the staff member promptly resigned.

Although the immediate problem of the staff member had been settled, the real issue was not resolved. During this intense time of personal crisis over Debbie's health, the opposition group did not relent. Instead, they seemed more determined than ever to remove Frank as pastor of Pleasant Hill Baptist Church. At the monthly business meetings, Frank was subjected to severe criticism and caustic and inaccurate remarks by the opposition. Only through God's grace was he able to deflect those comments with a smile and a polite "thank you." In the midst of the storm, God was giving Frank strength and encouragement, sometimes in unusual ways.

One particularly strange incident brought Frank a strong sense of God's assurance. Because the church was close to the interstate, drifters looking for a handout often came around. Frank sometimes was amused at the elaborate stories they would concoct. Therefore, when two strangers showed up proclaiming they had a message from God, he was naturally skeptical. One of them was blind, and the other had shaggy hair and torn clothes—not exactly how Frank would expect someone with a heavenly message to look. However, when the shaggy-haired man began to tell Frank in detail about his wife's illness and the trouble at the church, he was startled. There appeared to be no way the man could have known such specifics. From a bag he was carrying, the stranger pulled out a loaf of French bread and some grape juice. He insisted that the pastor have the Lord's Supper with him and his blind companion, and Frank agreed. The stranger then proceeded to pray in a manner that brought the presence of the Lord to Frank in a special way. Before he left, he assured Frank that if he remained faithful in preaching the Word of God, then "He will take care of your wife and the problems of the church. . . . The church may be emptied, but He'll fill it again with His people."[2] After the prayer, the man who had prayed put the juice and the bread back into the bag and, along with his companion, quickly walked out the door never to be seen by the pastor again. The pastor later described the event as an "Abraham thing, that is 'a time of testing' and that I knew I had entertained angels unaware."

> ". . . I knew I had entertained angels unaware."

At the church, the situation was moving toward a showdown. The opposition group as well as the supporters had made known their positions, but the key to the outcome of the crisis was actually a third group. These members were watching the pastor closely in order to decide which side they would support. How would he hold up in the midst of the overwhelming crises he was facing? His ability to keep his poise during the stormy business meetings represented a turning point. As Frank related, "Everybody knew that I was in the darkest spot that I could be in. . . . They decided that if that is how I handled the pressure that came at me, then they were willing to follow my leadership." This group became the key in determining the future of the church.

When Frank read the resignation letter of the staff member to the church, he was hopeful "that I could put it all behind me so I could focus on Debbie." Frank was dealing with the very difficult radiation and chemotherapy treatments that Debbie was undergoing. Unfortunately, the further decline of his wife's health only seemed to embolden his critics. The pastor and the deacon chairman met with three men who claimed to represent others. They demanded Frank's resignation, and gave four reasons. (1) Because of Debbie's situation, he could not be effective as a pastor. (2) He preached with power and anointing. (3) He was too good at reaching people in the community. (4) They thought he had talked about someone in one of his sermons.

In the proposal to terminate the staff member, Frank had arranged to give a generous severance. However, the group of three men wanted to terminate Frank from his position as pastor without any severance. They did offer a vague commitment to support Frank's ministry if he went into evangelism. Given what he considered to be the absurdity of their reasons for him to resign, Frank interpreted this gesture as disingenuous.

Frank and his supporters knew his opponents would bring a motion at the next business meeting that the congregation terminate him as the pastor. Because numerous members turned out for the previous meeting to consider the staff member's termination, the active deacons asked Frank whether he wanted them to "pack the place" with pastor supporters. Frank decided to take the high road and declined. Instead, something happened that Frank was convinced was further confirmation that God would take care of him. He received a call from the very person his opponents had falsely accused him of talking about in his sermons. She was one of the senior ladies in the church and was extremely respected. Assuring her pastor that the congregation would not vote him out, she single-handedly packed the business meeting with pastor supporters.

The dynamics of the business meeting turned strongly in favor of the pastor. The man who was to bring the motion against the pastor had been the kindergarten student of the woman who led the support for the pastor. Feeling the gaze of his former kindergarten teacher, he excused himself from bringing the motion. When the opponents made the motion, the criticism of the pastor seemed trite and far-fetched. For instance, one person leveled charges that the pastor had visited his house only twice

and only twice had asked about his terminally ill mother-in-law, who lived
in West Virginia. On the other hand, far more members stood to give a
strong testimony of how Frank had given excellent pastoral care to them
and their families in their times of need. When the vote came, the margin
was more than four to one in favor of the pastor.

Although the vote had gone favorably, the church crisis on top of
Debbie's condition had taken its toll on Frank. He later admitted, while
sitting in his office after the vote, "I was still low." When a couple of deacons met with him and asked what he would like to do, he responded that
he "would love to go and start a church that didn't have all that baggage."
Soon a group of 130 was ready to go with the pastor. They met every
Tuesday for a month. The group raised money and set a date for starting.

The Friday before the first Sunday for the new church, Frank was
deep in prayer. Prostrating himself before the Lord, he thanked Him for
the opportunity to start a new church. At that point, Frank was startled
by an "audible voice from the Lord." The voice said that God had not
called him to start a church. Instead, he was to continue as pastor of this
church. If Frank would stay faithful, the church would be emptied; but
then God would "fill it right back." The latter assurance echoed what the
stranger had said to him a few weeks before. After this revelation, Frank
told the group that was ready to start the church that they could go ahead
with his blessing, but God had not released him from Pleasant Hill. Their
response was that they were staying with their pastor.

The next Sunday was a watershed moment for Pleasant Hill Baptist
Church. Filled with passion about God's direction, Frank preached "How
to Build a Thriving Church." The last emphasis of the message was on the
importance of the unity of the church with everyone working in a coop-
erative spirit. At this point, Frank told them "what God had asked him to
say." Some of them had not followed the pastor's leadership, "and God's
word to them was that they move their membership." Frank offered
to meet with them afterward to give them suggestions for churches to
which they could move. The result fulfilled the first part of the revelation.
Within three weeks, Pleasant Hill had lost 170 members. For six months,
Frank preached in an auditorium with many empty pews.

Thankfully, the other part of the revelation also was coming to frui-
tion. In the weeks prior to the showdown business meeting, additions to

the church membership had virtually stopped. However, on the Sunday morning when Frank shared the message on "How to Build a Thriving Church," 25 people joined. In the year following the message, the church baptized 178 and had 192 other additions. The attendance more than doubled. It was the first of more than 24 years of remarkable growth. Under Frank's leadership, Pleasant Hill Baptist Church eventually relocated and became North Metro First Baptist Church. Today the church has an auditorium that seats 2,500 and multiple support facilities for Bible study and ministry. The congregation has become a megachurch with an attendance more than 10 times larger than it had at the time of its greatest trial. For Frank, the confirmation of the word he received was unmistakable. The conflict had emptied the church, but God had filled it far beyond what it had ever been before and more than anyone at Pleasant Hill could have dreamed.

Beyond the Story: Leadership Lessons

Walking through the Valley

Less than one year after the vote to terminate Frank and the mass exodus of members, Frank walked through the valley of losing his beloved wife Debbie. In his book, *Trusting God's Heart*, Frank shared the trial of Debbie's 27-month battle with the terminal brain tumor. He recalled the words of comfort shared to him at Debbie's funeral by a close friend and fellow pastor, Ike Reighard. Reighard had experienced a devastating loss a few years earlier when in childbirth both his wife and baby perished. Reighard quoted the words of C. H. Spurgeon, who in the midst of his own time of trial had learned that "when you cannot trace His hand, that's when you must learn to trust His heart."[3] In the midst of a crisis within a crisis, Frank felt pressed beyond his strength. He had no choice but to trust God or collapse.

Being overwhelmed was not something Frank often experienced. Frank is the type referred to as a man's man. This persona, combined with people skills, exudes a self-confidence and strength that instantly identifies him as a leader whom others want to follow. He is a gifted communicator with a great passion for souls. As a result, he had been successful in growing churches, whether in the bayous of Louisiana or in Metro Atlanta. Yet none of his talents or strengths could heal Debbie or make the opposition at the church go away. For Debbie's healing, he knew that he must humbly depend on God. He followed the scriptural teaching of Jas 5:14–15 and with the "elders" put her into God's hands. Because he did not want anything to interfere with the intercession for her healing, Frank related, "If there was any point in my life that I was very pure, it was during the crisis, because I was praying for Debbie's healing." The intimacy Frank found with God for the crisis with Debbie's health also provided him the strength he needed to withstand the pressure at the church. The result was counterintuitive but spiritually in tune with the promises of Scripture.

Assurance of the Call

Flowing out of the foundational and foremost issue of spiritual strength, other important leadership actions and perspectives helped Frank mitigate the crisis. One was his sense that God called him to pastor there. Pleasant Hill was a church that Frank had known well before he went to seminary. When the door opened for him to go there as pastor, he felt the call was providential. But initially the conflict appeared to derail his vision of a great church that would reach the surrounding community. When the additions to the church had dribbled to virtually none, it seemed unlikely that the church would become what Frank had envisioned. At his lowest point, starting a new church seemed to be the logical answer. However, an unmistakable word from the Lord assured him that God had called him to be the pastor of Pleasant Hill and that was where he should stay. Through the years, opportunities for highly prized pastorates and denominational positions came to Frank. During those times, the bedrock assurance forged in the crisis within a crisis removed any potential restlessness. His assurance might not have been as strong without the trials.

Grace and Strength

A key to overcoming the crisis in the church was the manner in which Frank handled the opposition. Privately, Frank was hurting from the caustic criticism and outright falsehoods. Yet he maintained a gracious demeanor to the opposition. When the conclusive information surfaced that required the termination of the staff member, Frank invited the inactive deacons to take part in the decision. His willingness to change tactics and take the risk of an inclusive strategy was successful in resolving the issue with the staff member. However, when including the opposition proved unsuccessful in defusing their fervor, Frank stood firm. His graciousness to the opposition did not restrain his resoluteness when it was required. He refused to resign under pressure, and he did not compromise his vision of the church in an attempt to placate the opposition.

Hindsight

Every leader has to make difficult decisions without the benefit of knowing all the ramifications. Frank freely admits in hindsight that he would have done some things differently. He felt that delaying the termination of the staff member by giving a six-month probation period only postponed the inevitable. Although well intended, the plan to start a new church was carried farther than it should have been without a definitive word from the Lord. Perhaps perceiving the signals from members who were playing "the game" of refusing to take church positions could have prevented the all-out conflict that resulted in a number of people leaving. With more understanding and less posturing by both sides, some who left might have caught the vision and been a part of the growth to come. When faced with difficult choices, a leader cannot possibly know all the potential outcomes of every decision. But the Christian leader has the comfort that the providential declaration of Rom 8:28 is true. When Frank Cox could not trace the hand of God, he was able to trust His heart. He not only survived "the two black clouds" but also received new blessings.

New Blessings

Today Frank Cox is enjoying the fruit of 29 years of ministry at the same church and has served in numerous denominational positions at the highest levels. Even more fulfilling has been the blessing of his family. Approximately three months before Debbie died, she told Frank,

North Metro First Baptist Church worshipping in the new facility. PHOTO SUB-
MITTED BY NORTH METRO FIRST BAPTIST CHURCH.

"I am not going to make it much longer. I want you to know that God has
already revealed that to me. I also want you to know I am praying for the
girl who will come into your life to love and care for you and Stephen."[4]
That girl would be the former Mary Roderick, now Frank's wife of 22
years. Stephen, who was only four at the time of Debbie's death, serves
with his father on the staff at North Metro First Baptist Church. Frank
and Mary have been blessed with the birth of two children, Jonathan and
Kristen. Like Job of old, Frank has seen God bring new blessings out of
the deepest of trials.

Questions for Further Thought

1. What are some reasons that it is difficult to change the culture of a declining church without experiencing conflict? Can change happen without conflict, or is it a necessary element for change to take place?

2. What would have been some effective countermeasures to "the game" the opposition was playing?

3. When change becomes personified, how can the leader redirect criticism to the issues at hand?

4. What were some of the dynamics in the attempted forced termination that apparently raised the level of conflict?

5. What were the risks of the co-optation strategy (bringing the opposition into the decision-making process) the pastor used in including the inactive deacons in the decision to terminate the staff member? In what ways did the co-optation strategy possibly help defeat the motion to terminate the pastor? What were some possible reasons the strategy succeeded?

Jonathan, Frank, Stephen, Kristen, Mary, Brooke (Stephen's wife). PHOTO SUBMITTED BY FRANK COX.

6. What are some strategies that might have kept the conflict from reaching the intense level that it did?

7. What possible impact did Debbie's terminal illness have on the manner in which the church dealt with its internal conflict? What can be the effects of multiple crises on a church and its leadership?

8. What role did shared leadership play in this situation? How did it help and hurt? How could shared leadership have strengthened the ministry of the church during this crisis? What were the dangers to those who were willing to stand with the pastor as leaders? What were the dangers of not standing with him?

Notes

1. F. Cox, *Trusting God's Heart: Finding Peace in Times of Sorrow* (Friendswood, TX: Baxter Press, 2000), 61.

2. Ibid., 91–92.

3. Ibid., 126–27.

4. Ibid., 153.

PART III

Help and Hope

Titanic lifeboat is half full as it pulls alongside the rescue ship Carpathia. PHOTO FROM THE LIBRARY OF CONGRESS.

Chapter 9

Leadership Lifeboats:
Help in Coping with Crises

"But Moses asked of God, 'Who am I that I should go to Pharaoh and that I should bring the Israelites out of Egypt?' He answered, 'I will certainly be with you.'" Exodus 3:11–12a

The High Stakes of Crisis Leadership

Shortly before midnight on the fateful evening of April 14, 1912, the *Titanic* struck an iceberg, which resulted in her sinking early the next morning. Of the approximately 2,200 people on board, only slightly more than 700 survived. It was a catastrophic crisis of the highest magnitude. Numerous errors led to the tragedy. However, most if not all of the passengers could have survived if not for a grievous neglect. The *Titanic* did not have an adequate number of lifeboats. Regulations required the *Titanic* to have a lifeboat capacity equal to the ship's capacity of over 3,500 people. The ship carried enough for a little less than 1,200. Even worse, in the hurry of the crew to launch the boats and with a concern for overfilling, the boats were not loaded to capacity. Thus, hundreds more could have been saved just by fully utilizing the lifeboats that were available. As the picture at the beginning of this chapter shows, some lifeboats were barely half full. From this inexcusable blunder, two primary lessons for leadership emerge. First, leaders must be prepared as much as possible for crises. Second, when a crisis occurs, they must maximize every resource at their disposal. In a figurative way, both leaders and constituents need plenty of lifeboats, and they must employ them fully. In such times, the survival of a ministry depends on it.

> *Leadership is always on trial, but never more so than during a catastrophic event.*

Leadership is always on trial, but never more so than during a catastrophic event. If "everything rises or falls on leadership,"[1] leaders also tend to rise or fall during a crisis, especially a catastrophic one. If leaders distinguish themselves in such moments, they will reap a higher level of trust and respect. The crisis actually can accelerate the normal period required for the leader to establish deep trust among constituents. Effective crisis management can "provide opportunities to strengthen the organization."[2] On the other hand, if leaders falter, they may never have the opportunity to regain the trust to lead.

Seven Stylistic Competencies

Crises come in many forms. But in the midst of these experiences are some common dimensions of leadership that we can identify and examine. Leadership literature often refers to *leadership style* as reflecting tendencies of leaders in terms of their approaches and characteristics. We also use the term *stylistic competency* because it reflects not just the manner of a leader but also the need for particular skills. In our case studies, we discovered that seven stylistic competencies were particularly important to ministry leadership in a time of crisis. To use the *Titanic* analogy, they serve as *leadership lifeboats*. They provide the means for a congregation or ministry organization not only to survive but also in some instances even to thrive in the midst of extremely trying circumstances. We believe that these leadership lifeboats are channels of help through which God empowers leaders in such perilous moments. In this chapter, we explore some of the ways these stylistic competencies are relevant in times of crisis and in the normative challenges of leadership.

Each of the seven stylistic competencies focuses on a way leaders can inspire others to follow. (1) Through modeling spiritual vitality, *spiritual leaders* motivate God's people to fulfill God's purposes. (2) *Assuring leaders* provide hope and confidence to constituents in the midst of difficult circumstances. (3) *Visionary leaders* communicate the ultimate purpose of an organization in such a vivid and appealing manner that followers not only understand that purpose but also are motivated to embrace it with passionate commitment. (4) *Decisive leaders* discern the need for an immediate decision and have the fortitude to execute it in a manner that temporarily may require an authoritative style. (5) *Empathetic leaders* connect with constituents in such a compassionate way that they know the leader genuinely cares for their difficulties, sufferings, and losses. (6) *Empowering leaders* equip and enable others to employ their talents and abilities to the fullest. (7) *Creative leaders* respond with innovation and intuition to find solutions to problems and challenges they cannot solve through previously established means. The stylistic competency a leader employs should emerge from intimate knowledge of the followers as well as insight about the prevailing situation.

Understanding the Biblical Stances as Foundational

The expression of each of these stylistic competencies rests on a substantive foundation. Undergirding the leadership lifeboat competencies are two primary biblical concepts that we call *leadership stances.* Robert Dale distinguished between stance and style: "A leadership stance provides a foundation, a basic position and reason for exercising leadership. Style, on the other hand, is a leader's manner of expressing initiative, a distinctive fashion of leading."[3] These two biblical stances, *transformational leadership* and *servant leadership*, comprise the foundational nature of how followers of Christ should lead. Depending on the context, leaders may need to adjust the employment of stylistic competencies. Yet regardless of which stylistic competency leaders may exhibit in a situation, they always should act out of the stances of transformational and servant leadership.

The teachings and actions of Jesus contained a strong emphasis on transformational and servant leadership. He defined and demonstrated the very nature of these two biblical stances. Jesus taught, "If anyone wants to be first, he must be last of all and servant of all" (Mark 9:35). In washing the disciples' feet, Jesus left an indelible impression on them. He declared, "For I have given you an example that you also should do just as I have done for you" (John 13:15). However, the ultimate purpose of servant leadership is not only to serve but also to see transformational results. Jesus did not come just to serve but to be a "ransom for many" in order to transform His followers into His likeness. Jesus came for a rescue mission, a transformational purpose—"to seek and to save that which is lost" (Luke 19:10, NASB). Likewise, other New Testament writings are replete with this emphasis. Paul declared, "Therefore, if anyone is in Christ, he is a new creation; old things have passed away, and look, new things have come" (2 Cor 5:17).

Not only are the stances of servant leadership and transformational leadership the primary ones found in the New Testament, but leadership writers have also discussed them extensively. Servant leadership theory often is associated with Robert T. Greenleaf, and likewise transformational leadership theory with James McGregor Burns. Both wrote seminal books concerning these approaches to leadership. Greenleaf focused on how the leader was a "*servant first*" and that leadership influence was a natural outcome of a servant commitment.[4] Burns contrasted transformational leadership, which "seeks to satisfy higher needs . . . engages the full person . . . [and] converts followers into leaders and moral agents," with task-centered transactional leadership, which centers on "exchanging one thing for another."[5] However, for ministerial leadership the key focus should not be primarily on the secular versions of these theories but on the biblical teachings concerning servant and transformational leadership.

Synergism in the Biblical Stances

The biblical stances of transformational leadership and servant leadership interact in dynamic, synergistic relationship: together they produce more than the sum total of their individual benefits. Either stance has the potential to produce positive outcomes, but they are much more effective together. Following the biblical pattern, a transformational purpose is the motive of Christian leadership and service is the mode. The synergism is reciprocal in that optimum transformational leadership results in service and optimum servant leadership results in transformation in both the one who serves and those who are served. Additionally, and very importantly, they also serve as a balance to prevent excesses. Especially in times of crisis, leaders sorely need this dynamic synergism and balance.

> *Following the biblical pattern, a transformational purpose is the motive of Christian leadership and service is the mode.*

The balance of the servant mode is particularly critical when facing the potential excesses of visionary leadership. Transformational leadership and visionary leadership are closely related. Transformational leaders *"create* a vision" and *"communicate* that vision to others."[6] Unfortunately, Christian transformational leaders who hold the conviction that their visions for the ministry are from God may also believe that, as a result, their followers should not question them. This mind-set may degenerate into the view that, because God has chosen them, they have the right to impose their will.[7] They rationalize that their autocratic methods are necessary to carry out God's purpose. Church history is replete with examples. A major crisis only increases the potential for this type of leadership. Servant leadership serves as a check against this aberrant thought by reminding transformational leaders who they are. They are not to be despots their followers must serve but servants to those they lead.

At the same time, without the balance of transformational leadership, the leader who operates out of a servant leadership stance may
exhibit excesses that lead to poor results and subsequent discouragement. In the local church setting, a common occurrence among pastors illustrates the potential misuse of the servant leadership mode. Let
us call our subject Brother Bob. Brother Bob's parishioners love him
because he is truly a servant. He is always there with needed pastoral
care. Brother Bob goes to the extreme in meeting the most minor of
needs of his congregation. He even ministers to the relatives and friends
of church members. Unfortunately, Brother Bob's preaching suffers
because he lacks the time to have the highest level of sermon preparation. He also fails to give the needed attention to leadership issues
because he does not want to make anyone angry but prefers to "minister to the flock." Although everyone loves Brother Bob, his leadership
stance presents a problem. The church is in decline. This pastor has
failed to realize that servant leadership includes developing believers
for the work of the ministry. It also means making the tough decisions
that will keep the church on course with its transformational mission.
Servant leaders are to replicate themselves in a way that allows others
to experience transformation. Servant leaders should seek transformational outcomes in the lives of the people they serve.

Stylistic Competencies in the Ministry of Jesus

Jesus not only serves as the perfect model in employing the biblical
stances of transformational leadership and servant leadership, but He is
also the perfect pattern for utilizing the needed stylistic competencies. As
the supreme spiritual leader and an example in all things, Jesus urged his
disciples to follow Him (John 12:26). His prayer life was so vibrant that
it inspired His disciples to request, "Lord, teach us to pray" (Luke 11:1).
Matthew 28:19–20 records Jesus, as a visionary leader, casting the ultimate vision. John 14:1–3 depicts Jesus as the assuring leader, while John
11:35 shows that He is the empathetic leader. The Sermon on the Mount
reveals Jesus as the decisive leader, proclaiming "But I tell you" (Matt
5:22). Matthew 10:1 reveals Jesus as the empowering leader who com-
missions the disciples and gives them authority. Finally, Jesus exhibited

the ultimate creative leader quality in a new and radically different message akin to putting "new wine into old wineskins" (Mark 2:22). The practice of these leadership stylistic competencies is efficacious. Yet ministry leaders have a greater reason for employing them. In doing so, they "follow in His steps" (1 Pet 2:21).

Utilizing the Seven Stylistic Competencies

These seven stylistic competencies do not exist in isolation. They affect each other in three ways. First, like transformational and servant leadership, they have a synergistic relationship. Strength in one area enhances effectiveness in the other areas. For example, strong spiritual leadership augments the employment of all the other characteristics. In a number of ways, the ability to employ the seven competencies becomes a force multiplier. Practiced together, their impact is greater than the apparent sums of their individual benefits.

> *. . . the ability to employ the seven competencies becomes a force multiplier.*

A second aspect is that these competencies are effective when employed in the appropriate context. As the writer of Ecclesiastes declared, "There is an occasion for everything, and a time for every activity under heaven" (Eccl 3:1). The leader must discern which quality fits the circumstances. For instance, as important as visionary leadership is, there are moments in a crisis when people do not want to hear about the grand scheme of things. Instead, they need an empathetic and assuring leader. At age 30, I learned this lesson through becoming the pastor of a church that had lost a large number of members as the result of a severe congregational split. Initially, my preaching focused on the exciting visionary possibilities of the church. What I said was very true, but at the time most of the members were too hurt to think about grand visions. The author of Prov 27:14 warned, "If one blesses his neighbor with a loud voice early in the morning, it will be counted as a curse to him." In other words, even a good intention manifested at the wrong time can be ineffective. On the other hand, the right action at the right moment can be like "gold apples on a silver tray" (Prov 25:11). Over the course of time as I also preached the therapeutic or healing aspects of God's Word, the congregation once again was able to embrace a renewed vision.

A third aspect to the relationship of these qualities is also similar to the interaction between transformational leadership and servant leadership in that they bring balance to each other. Leaders naturally will be stronger in some of these seven areas and weaker in others. The use of all these aspects reduces two risks: overusing a strength and failing to compensate for a weakness. However, the danger of overuse does not apply equally to these characteristics. For instance, a leader cannot be excessive in spiritual leadership in accordance with the biblical model. But it is possible to practice excessively some of the stylistic competencies, such as decisive leadership in the midst of a crisis. Although this quality is a strength, the constituents likely will perceive the leaders to be authoritative if they do not balance decisiveness with empathetic leadership and a willingness to empower others. As Bob Kaplan and Rob Kaiser observed, "A strength overused can be as ineffective as a strength underused. In other words, overusing a strength is under performance."[8] Thus, a strength that is not balanced with other skills may become a negative.

Fortunately, the strengths of some competencies may at least partly mitigate the weaknesses of other areas. Yet in ministerial leadership, balance is critical. In particular, in non-crisis situations the lack of urgency means that constituents are less likely to be patient with the shortcomings of the leader. Additionally, in recent years, congregations have developed higher expectations of ministerial leadership. Therefore, a nimble adeptness at employing multiple leadership competencies has become even more vital regardless of the context or circumstances.

Spiritual Leadership

Spiritual leadership is motivating God's people to fulfill God's purposes through leaders who model spiritual vitality.

Steven Sample observed, "In the end the failure of crisis leadership is a profound failure of ethical and spiritual leadership of the highest forms."[9] Douglas Brinkley adopted a similar view in his critique of the handling of the aftermath of Hurricane Katrina in 2005. Brinkley cited numerous leadership failures on the national, state, and local government levels that he said were a combination of indifference, incompetence, and reprehensible ethical standards. One example among many was his scathing denunciation of the mayor of New Orleans for failing to order an earlier evacuation because he was concerned about the loss of tourism dollars more than the potential loss of lives.[10] Conversely, in the case studies in this book effective spiritual leadership was a key factor in the ability to cope with the crisis. In Christian ministry, we assume that impeccable ethical standards are part of spiritual leadership. A ministry leader should be able to declare with Paul, "Imitate me, as I also imitate Christ" (1 Cor 11:1). For this reason, in our definition we note the importance of the spiritual vitality of leaders as well as the motivation they provide.

In *Spiritual Leadership*, Henry and Richard Blackaby made a concerted effort to distinguish between spiritual leadership and secular leadership. They noted, "Spiritual leadership is moving people on to God's agenda."[11] The distinction involves both purpose and methodology. Spiritual leadership involves transformational leadership in the development of disciples. It is growing God's people "with a stature measured by Christ's fullness" (Eph 4:13). Spiritual leadership is also servant leadership in that it overrides any personal agenda. As J. Oswald Sanders observed, "The true spiritual leader is focused on the service he or she can render to God and other people, not the residuals and perks of high office or holy title."[12] Therefore, the spiritual vitality of leaders and their ability to lead their followers to a deeper level of spiritual vitality are key to the effective practice of the biblical stances of transformational and servant leadership.

> *Catastrophic crises do not announce themselves.*

In this book's case studies, the spiritual vitality of the leaders that enabled them to lead effectively prior to the crisis was especially essential in the midst of the acute trials. Catastrophic crises do not announce themselves. While a spiritual renewal may occur as the result of the crisis, the critical initial reactions as well as the overwhelming number of long-term coping responses require a spiritual foundation built prior to the event. The catastrophic crisis is a time for drawing from a deep reservoir of previous spiritual vitality. Such was the case when under great stress Frank Cox experienced a distinct revelation from God. In the same manner, the deep faith of Cindy Winters enabled her to speak powerfully at her husband's funeral. Rather than being filled with bitterness toward the one who had murdered her husband, instead she called the funeral a "celebration day" for the ministry of her husband and the certainty that he was in heaven.[13] Later, in national interviews, she spoke of her forgiveness for the perpetrator and her supreme concern that he would come to know forgiveness and salvation in Christ. She even expressed a desire to minister to his family.[14] As a result, a terrible tragedy became a nationally publicized expression of the transformational power of the Christian faith.

> *. . . spiritual leaders raise the level of the spiritual vitality of their followers.*

Out of their transformational-servant leadership stance, spiritual leaders raise the level of the spiritual vitality of their followers. In a crisis it is vital that the entire congregation or ministry organization have an advance reservoir of spiritual insight, not just the leaders. Teaching that insight and reinforcing that perspective during the crisis are important tasks of the spiritual leader. At First Baptist Church of Lindale, the pastor had established a foundation of expository preaching that taught his congregation to have a faith perspective. Yet during the crisis, it was important for him to reinforce that foundation with a series from Nehemiah. Chris Burns credited some of the resiliency of his congregation to a wonderful spiritual outpouring in a two-week extended revival that had occurred some months before the tornado. However, the message he brought on Easter Sunday after the tornado was critical. At First Baptist Church, Oak Forest, the commitment of the spiritually mature kept the church from succumbing to those who were ready to make plans for the demise of the congregation. Throughout the crisis period, the interim pastors and others encouraged them in their hope that the church would recover.

With both the leaders and the constituents, two key spiritual perspectives were vital for morale. One was the belief they should not blame God for what had happened. Although the question of why the catastrophic events or circumstances had occurred was unanswerable, they interpreted the crises as the suffering and trials of living in this world. A second key perspective was that God was working in the midst of the crisis. As Kenneth P. Yusko and Harold Goldstein noted, in a crisis "many things may be out of the leader's control. . . . Even if a leader takes the 'correct' action, there is no guarantee of success."[15] Yet, often in this book's case studies, the victims had faith that God would give the strength and grace to endure the trial. For the most part, the leaders and their constituents embraced the principle of Rom 8:28 that God would bring some good results out of the trial.

In this book's case studies, the spiritual growth that ensued was one dimension of the fulfillment of the promise that God can work a good result even in the midst of catastrophe. Robert Clinton observed that in a major crisis "the leader sees that his only hope is in God. He experiences God in a new way in the crisis."[16] In a catastrophic crisis, everyone involved has the potential for either finding a deeper level of spiritual vitality or becoming spiritually disillusioned. The practice of the biblical stances of transformational and servant leadership by the leader will be a prime determinative of the outcome.

Assuring Leadership

Assuring leadership is providing hope and confidence to constituents in the midst of difficult circumstances.

Crises inevitably have moments when the assurance of the leader is pivotal. On September 14, 2001, three days after the terrorist attack on the twin towers of the World Trade Center in New York City, President George Bush stood on the rubble with a bullhorn in hand and offered assurance and encouragement to the workers and all Americans. Whatever the various views of political pundits may have been about the president's actions, it was a critical leadership moment for inspiring confidence to a shocked nation. On the contrary, exhibiting weakness in such a moment can be disastrous. During Hurricane Katrina, television interviews showed the mayor of New Orleans with a glaring lack of composure and the police superintendent crying. Fair or unfair, such behavior proved disconcerting to the citizens of the city and severely undermined the leadership of these two public officials. Likewise, one media source characterized Louisiana Governor Kathleen Blanco as "more like a woman at a funeral than a pillar of support."[17] Her inability to inspire was a key reason for her steep fall in popularity as the result of the Katrina catastrophe.

One of the worst mistakes a leader can make in such circumstances is to "bunker in." Instead, history contains numerous examples that high visibility for leaders is critical in crisis times. Prime Minister Winston Churchill endeared himself to the British public by frequently being present on the scene after the devastation of German bombing attacks. The soldiers of Julius Caesar and Napoleon revered them for their courage in placing themselves at risk by personally leading the troops into the heat of battle.[18]

Timothy Laniak observed, "One of the primary metaphors by which biblical authors conceptualized leadership is shepherding."[19] Like a good shepherd, the ministry leader does not abandon the flock to hibernate during the crisis. Ezekiel 34:5 warns that God's people "were scattered for lack of a shepherd." Ministry leaders must be willing to stand with their people in the roughest moments of the crisis

> *Ministry leaders must be willing to stand with their people in the roughest moments of the crisis or chaos will result.*

or chaos will result. It epitomizes the commitment to serve. In pastoral ministry, the image of the shepherd among the sheep brings calmness to the flock. In the case studies in this book, the physical presence of the leaders and their remarkable composure became an initial rallying point for recovery. They were on the scene early and often throughout the crisis. The competency of these leaders to give assurance to their constituents kept morale from plummeting and laid the foundation for eventual recovery.

Eric K. Stern observed that early in a crisis it is absolutely critical for leaders to be able to get their bearings and to see clearly through the "'fog' of crisis."[20] They must rise higher than even their own emotions and feelings seemingly would allow. Meeting this challenge in tumultuous moments takes extraordinary fortitude. In various ways, the leaders in our study received an inner assurance that God would give them the wisdom and strength to lead. They could say with Paul, "I am able to do all things through Him who strengthens me" (Phil 4:13). His provision for the moment flowed out of their devotional lives and personal encounters with God during the crises. As a result, by God's grace the leaders were able to project a confidence that transferred to their constituents in a transformational manner.

As with other stylistic competencies, good communication is essential for assuring leadership. John Kotter posited that leaders underestimate the need to communicate by a factor of 10, or 100, or even 1,000.[21] Kotter was not referring to the intensity of a crisis, when communication is even more critical. A crisis often spawns a frantic desire for information. As a result, the dissemination of information in a prompt and truthful manner is imperative. Leaders may vary widely in their communication skills, but nothing is more vital than being truthful. Anything less compounds the crisis, and in the end the truth will usually become apparent.

Ian I. Mitroff observed the contrast in the outcomes of crises when leaders told the truth from the beginning versus employing an initial strategy of deception. Specifically, Mitroff noted the truthfulness of the classic crisis case of Johnson & Johnson in the infamous tampering of Tylenol with poison in 1982 that killed several people in different locations across the country. The company fully disclosed what it knew and moved quickly to recall millions of bottles of Tylenol. As a result, Johnson & Johnson continued to thrive after experiencing a catastrophe that could have caused its demise. In contrast, President Bill Clinton had no choice but to retract his initial denial in the Monica Lewinsky scandal. The resulting damage to his presidency was extensive and irrevocable.[22]

The link between a leader's ability to communicate assurance and the personal integrity of the leader is clear. For over a decade, the research of James Kouzes and Barry Posner confirmed that the number one trait followers sought from the leader was honesty. People want to know whether the leader is being aboveboard with them.[23] No combination of strengths in any leadership skill or style can substitute for trust. Without it, the ministry leader has no moral basis to lead. Fortunately, at First Baptist Church, Shreveport, the pastor and minister of education and administration had established trust with each other, with the staff, and with the congregation. That trust permeated the various leadership levels of the church and was apparent in the congregation's decisions and actions in response to the tragic bus crash.

The integrity and devotion that flow from the spiritual leader's life provide the best foundation for issuing reassuring public communication in the intensity of the crisis. In such high-pressure situations, rehearsed answers are insufficient when leaders struggle to hide their actual feelings. As a result, for good or bad, crises often reveal publicly who the leader really is. When catastrophic events draw the attention of the news media, the stakes are even higher. One study noted that because of intensifying media focus, "crisis communication has come to rival operational decision making and action as the prime focus of attention for crisis managers."[24] For Jim Parker, the challenge of dealing with the overwhelming media interest was in some ways more intense than the logistics of the loss of the facilities. Yet because of his spiritual investment prior to the crisis, he was able to say, with integrity, that the church membership had already forgiven the arsonists.

In non-crisis times, the leadership stylistic competency of bringing an assuring presence is also a great asset. The well-timed appearance of the leader can provide a helpful boost to a particular aspect of the ministry organization and can serve as a much-needed affirmation or endorsement. In addition, the social interaction of such moments gives the assurance that the leader is "one of us" and understands us. Pastors who are visible and interactive with their members know the condition of their flock more intimately. Likewise, all leaders can enhance the feedback loop of valuable input from the grass roots of their organizations simply by being regularly present in the public settings of their organizations.

Visionary Leadership

Visionary leadership is the skill to communicate the ultimate purpose of an organization in such a vivid and appealing manner that followers not only understand that purpose but also are motivated to embrace it with passionate commitment.

In his extensive research on the effectiveness of various leadership styles, Daniel Goleman found that visionary leadership was consistently the most effective style.[25] Philip Lewis asserted, "Vision is fundamental to all leadership."[26] Effective visionary leaders are able to foster excitement and passion among constituents for the true purpose of the organization. They not only enable followers to understand the mission of the organization but also motivate them to be willing to sacrifice to achieve it. The ministry leader operates under the supreme vision cast by Christ and has the task of inspiring commitment to that vision among fellow believers.

> *"Vision is fundamental to all leadership."*

The visionary dimension of leadership requires leaders to express strategic direction in practical as well as idealistic terms. As Michael Useem opined, "Leadership is at its best when the vision is strategic, the voice persuasive, the results tangible."[27] Effective visionary leadership is not giving dreamy and lofty pronouncements, but rather it is connecting an inspiring purpose with reality. In the midst of the convoluted circumstances of a crisis, the visionary leader is able to set a course of action.[28] Marshall and Molly Sashkin noted that visionary leadership fulfills the leadership act of "making a difference."[29] Competency in the visionary style is particularly vital in a crisis because it is a time when leaders can ill afford to be ineffectual. In such challenging moments, the visionary leader can make a difference in several ways.

First, in a time of crisis, especially one of catastrophic intensity, there is a strong connection between the skill of visionary leadership and the assuring leader. When catastrophe strikes, the normative operational mode is no longer valid, and the future of the ministry is uncertain. In order to bring assurance, the leader must be able to continue to articulate the mission of the church or ministry. Otherwise, people can quickly lose focus. Ronald A. Heifetz observed that a major challenge for leaders "is to draw attention and then deflect it to the questions and issues that need to be faced."[30] In reminding followers of their mission, visionary leaders draw attention to the most urgent tasks. Having a purpose before them keeps a congregation from being distracted and diminishes the potential for discouragement. Visionary leaders keep hope alive and morale high.

Second, visionary leadership plays a vital role in minimizing conflict. In a catastrophic crisis, normal no longer exists. Predictably, there is immediate uncertainty about proper channels of authority. With new problems arising and with no established method of handling them, the usual plethora of opinions of how to proceed can quickly divide a congregation or ministry organization. All of these factors, combined with heightened emotion, greatly increase the chances for serious conflict. In response, the visionary leader provides a sense of direction. Even in the midst of trauma, visionary leadership can get people moving in the same direction again.

Third, as Kotter noted, visionary leadership helps keep alignment in the organization by providing a mental model that "simplifies hundreds or thousands of detailed decisions."[31] Reestablishing the common vision brings order in the midst of chaos and prevents the congregation or ministry from being thwarted by the myriads of distracting issues. The author of Prov 29:18 declared, "Without revelation people run wild." The Hebrew word *chazon* (translated "vision" in the NASB) "is commonly associated with the visions of the prophets."[32] In other words, if there is no revelation from God, then people go in every direction. It becomes like the condition found in Judges when "every man did what was right in his own eyes" (Judg 17:6, NASB). In contrast, when the ministry leader puts forth a biblical vision, it promotes a unity of purpose. By focusing on the big picture, people have less propensity to divert their energy to secondary matters that have potential to be divisive. The positive atmosphere that develops also minimizes the "well-intentioned dragons" (as Marshall

Shelley described some difficult congregational members) of opposition and factions.[33]

Fourth, visionary leadership during a crisis aids in the mobilization of the available resources. Crises are extremely taxing to those involved. Understandably, people are often numb, particularly if they have suffered great personal loss. Even if the catastrophic crisis did not directly affect them with a personal loss or affliction, they still may feel physically and emotionally depleted. Yet during a crisis their commitments and abilities can be of the most benefit. At this critical moment, visionary leaders are able to inspire followers to commit to a cause greater than their own individual agendas. Peter Senge observed, "Given a choice, most people opt for pursuing a lofty goal, not only in times of crisis, but at all times."[34] Thus, by "pursuing a lofty goal," a visionary leader precipitates the release of a tremendous potential of commitment, creativity, and energy. In the case studies in this book, it was inspirational to observe how much people were able and willing to do in the midst of a crisis in response to visionary leadership.

Fifth, visionary leadership also may enhance the relationship with the community outside the congregation. The leader who communicates the bigger picture that the church can make an impact on the community can foster an opportunity for positive relationships. At Bethel Baptist Church, those positive relationships were a key factor in the ability of the church to thrive in the midst of the devastation of losing their facilities. In the case of First Baptist Church, Oak Forest, the fact that the church had not been able to connect with the growing minority population of the community represented, to some degree, a deficiency in a vision for the potential of such a ministry. Concerning New Orleans Baptist Theological Seminary, the vision of being part of the restoration of the community became a strong motivation for the leadership to make the NOBTS campus operational as quickly as possible.

While a leader can blossom in the crucial area of visionary leadership because of a crisis, it is much more beneficial for the leader previously to have established the vision in strong fashion. For instance, when the arsonist destroyed Ashby Baptist Church, Jim Parker already had established a vision that extended beyond the building the church occupied. Being in an area with an increasing population and with the church experiencing significant growth, the congregation had planned to expand the auditorium. Parker freely admitted that the vision for these plans greatly helped the church to see beyond the destruction of the buildings to the greater purpose of a new facility. When someone donated 10 acres to help them relocate, the congregation viewed this provision as divine providence in working something good out of something bad. A biblically based vision gives the congregation a spiritual template to perceive divine provision and guidance in the midst of coping with the crisis.

In a variety of leadership contexts, a visionary stylistic competency has proven to be the most successful in achieving the purpose of the organization. A biblical vision will do the same and more for ministry, whether in the context of a crisis or in the normative challenges of leadership praxis. Yet the crisis brings a sense of urgency to the task. Jim Herrington, Mike Bonem, and James H. Furr observed, "Urgency is critical in the individual congregation. It creates a driving force that makes the organization willing to accept change."[35] In the midst of the crisis, the communication of the biblical vision by the visionary leader works in a transformational way as it underscores the exigency of the mission of the church.

Decisive Leadership

> *Decisive Leadership involves discerning the need for an immediate decision and having the fortitude to execute it in a manner that temporarily may require an authoritative style.*

Concerning leadership in the midst of a crisis, Gary Yukl noted, "In this kind of situation, subordinates expect the leader to be more assertive, directive, and decisive."[36] In some instances, the need for decisive leadership requires a more commanding approach. Positional rank in quasi-military fashion becomes the leader's optimum action. Goleman observed that the commanding style is most effective in the "emergency situation."[37] Sometimes called authoritative, autocratic, or coercive, leaders who use the commanding style unilaterally make decisions in a forceful manner. Because they do not attempt to build a consensus, these leaders can provide immediate decisions.

Without question, a crisis requires an adjustment from the normal mode of operational leadership. Constituents expect strong leadership in such cases as a matter of practical necessity. When a storm is approaching, there is no time to debate whether to evacuate. Likewise, when survival is at stake, there are often very short windows of opportunity to take advantage of certain resources. In order for Bethel Baptist Church to worship on Easter Sunday just four days after the tornado, Chris Burns had to decide immediately on the location for the service. Likewise, Chuck Kelley had to move quickly to employ a contractor in order to secure scant resources and maintain a challenging timetable for rebuilding the campus. Often, a Monday morning quarterbacking group will criticize the leader's decisions later, and hindsight has 20/20 vision. However, the consensus of followers generally favors a leader who is decisive in such situations versus one whose indecision squanders potential opportunities and resources.

Leaders who possess the stylistic competency of being decisive in crises should exercise great caution in employing the commanding mode in normal situations. In a non-crisis situation, a leader who employs the commanding style out of positional power can only hope at best to get compliance. Even in crises, it has a limited shelf life. Full commitment from constituents ultimately requires their buy-in. Paul was a decisive leader as demonstrated in Acts and his epistles. However,

> *Full commitment from constituents ultimately requires their buy-in.*

Paul also knew the importance of working through a process and building a consensus. Acts 15 records the decision of the Jerusalem Council where Paul worked together with the leaders of the Jerusalem church to produce a decision that was be acceptable to both Jewish and Gentile believers. The challenge for the leader is to know when to transition from a unilateral method to a more inclusive process of decision making. At Bethel Baptist Church, Randy Gunter initially formed an emergency team.

However, once the situation was stable, he discerned that he needed to move back toward the preexisting norms of decision making. The solicitation of feedback and openness to hear it are critical for the successful timing of this shift.

When the catastrophic crisis is not an immediate cataclysmic event but a situation that develops over time, the sense of emergency often is not present. If the sense of emergency is not present, tolerance for unilateral decision making is much lower. Therefore, the leader must show particular restraint in the use of the commanding style. For instance, both Tim Burnham and Frank Cox would have played into the hands of their opposition if they had frequently employed a commanding style. It would have reinforced the criticism that they were authoritarian rather than servant leaders. The challenges were not the result of one single event but conditions within the congregation that developed over time. Therefore, the congregation did not experience the confusion and shock in the same manner that would have resulted from a tragic event. Nonetheless, as Frank and Tim demonstrated, decisiveness was important. Yet there was time for them to be more process centered. In the same way, even in the normal flow of challenges, the leader must balance the decisiveness competency with consensus building. The decisive leader also must be an inclusive leader.

Empathetic Leadership

> *Empathetic leadership is connecting with constituents in such a compassionate way that they know the leader genuinely cares for their difficulties, sufferings, and losses.*

Whether in the context of a crisis or in the normative challenges of leadership, empathetic leadership is needed to balance the strong assertiveness of decisive leadership. Yukl observed that in a crisis a leader must ask "for sacrifices and make unpopular changes."[38] As a result, he posited that a leader also provides "encouragement and support to people who are vulnerable to the increased stress of changing, sharing hardships and sacrifices with followers."[39] This dimension goes beyond mere presence to the ability to connect with people in a compassionate way that demonstrates concerns about their suffering. Failure to do so greatly reduces the effectiveness of a leader.

In the Gulf of Mexico oil spill of 2010, British Petroleum CEO Tony Hayward told the media that he was anxious to solve the crisis so that he could get his life back. The media and the public seized on that statement as representing a self-serving attitude in the midst of such suffering and hardship that many were experiencing, especially those who had lost loved ones in the tragedy. Hayward was never able to recover his leadership after those remarks, and the board of directors eventually removed him as CEO. Even those who have been successful in the past at demonstrating empathetic leadership must be careful of the perceptions they may create.

Although President Bush received mostly praise for his bullhorn speech during the 9/11 crisis, the critics castigated him for what they felt was an initial disengagement from the dramatic events of Katrina. Later, the image of him viewing the destruction from high above in a plane further reinforced this perception. For the remainder of the crisis, the president and his administration could never completely absolve themselves of the view of many that they had been indifferent to the suffering from the catastrophe.

A number of leadership writers have identified empathetic leadership as critically important. Marshall and Molly Sashkin measured caring as one of the 10 essential characteristics on their widely used leadership profile.[40] Peter Salovey, David Caruso, Daniel Goleman, and others have listed empathy as a prominent aspect of both emotional and social intelligence.[41] Goleman, in particular, gave the distinction between "cognitive empathy," which is an intellectual recognition that someone is hurting, and genuine empathy, an emotional identification with the afflicted.[42]

The caring leader is congruent with the servant leader model advocated by Greenleaf. He maintained that servant leaders "have empathy and an unqualified acceptance" of the ones they serve.[43] If leaders are servants first, then their influence flows out of their sense of service and true empathy. From a business perspective, Paul T. P. Wong noted that servant leadership theory "emphasizes the importance of leadership motivation and postulates that most workers will respond positively to leaders who seek to serve."[44] Yet Greenleaf, who was a Quaker, did not advocate servant leadership that shows care and concern in order to gain leadership influence. Instead, leadership should result from the trust of those the leaders serve. Likewise, the motivation for Christian leaders to empathize is not for the influence it brings, but rather because Jesus taught His followers to "love your neighbor as yourself" (Matt 22:39).

When Chuck Kelley asked his administrative team what would be the best thing he could do when the victims returned to campus for the first time, they responded that he should go around in his car to hand out water and talk with them awhile. The practical reason was to encourage people to take a break from the sweltering heat. In reality, the outcome was something much greater. It was so impressive that the father of a student later thanked Kelley profusely for taking the time to give a bottle of water to his son and listen to him share his story. Kelley did not distribute the water or listen to gain the confidence of his constituents, but that is what occurred. Pastoral, empathetic leadership in the case studies in this book was indispensable for the acceptance of the leaders who had to make the hard decisions their positions demanded. In any circumstance, leaders who are concerned only with self-interest will have difficulty getting compliance from followers, much less commitment. Conversely, regardless of whether or not the setting is a crisis event, those leaders who demonstrate a Christlike compassion and care will find constituents much more receptive to their direction.

> *Empathy is not a quality that leaders can counterfeit easily.*

Empathy is not a quality that leaders can counterfeit easily. When a catastrophic crisis occurs, people can perceive whether the leader is merely looking for a "photo op" or is genuinely concerned. Ken Blanchard and Phil Hodges described the former as a "give a little, take a lot" attitude toward followers.[45] Ministry leaders should not have to try to manufacture the feeling of empathy, as emotional intelligence writers Caruso and Salovey suggested.[46] Instead, they have empathy because with Paul they can say, "I no longer live, but Christ lives in me" (Gal 2:20).

In the church setting, the pastoral care side of leadership is essential to prevent members from falling away. Catastrophic crises and even routine leadership challenges inevitably produce situations in which people are hurt. They may have been victims of a tragic event or embroiled in a conflict that either precipitated or resulted from the crisis. Either way, ministering to people is critical. Not only can pastoral ministry help prevent attrition, but also in several instances in our case studies, the extension of pastoral care reclaimed members.

In dealing with inevitable conflict, the reconciling leader must be able to empathize with the parties on each side. In the intensity of a crisis, it is more important than ever not to demonize the opposition. The minister must consider the perspective of Henry Wadsworth Longfellow, who opined that "if we could read the secret history of our enemies, we would find in each life a sorrow and suffering enough to disarm all of our hostility."[47] However, ministers should not naïvely think that all opposition is because of the suffering involved in the crisis. Some of it is volitional and independent of the crisis, even preexisting the crisis, and certainly malevolent in its intent. Neither should leaders allow their empathy to tempt them to compromise their principles. Leaders also must be on the lookout for potential antagonists who may use crisis events as an opportunity to gain power and influence. Nonetheless, the ability to empathize even with opponents allows for reconciliation both during and after the crisis.

The reconciling effect is one of the most important aspects of empathetic leadership. On a number of occasions in the case studies in this book, reconciliation was a vital part of overcoming the detrimental effects of the crisis. Reconciliation was a key factor in enabling Tim Burnham to see the attendance return to 90 percent of its pre-crisis level. First Baptist Church of Maryville was able to forgive and move forward. In so doing, these ministries truly manifested the transformational-servant leadership stance found in the earthly ministry of Jesus Christ.

Empowering Leadership

Empowering leadership is the ability to equip and enable others to employ their talents and abilities to the fullest.

Leading and managing in a catastrophic crisis can be overwhelming. The pace is so intense that leaders are likely to become exhausted if they do not share the load. The skill sets that are required for a crisis can be particularly taxing. Delegation and team building become not a luxury of choice but a necessity for survival. Bill George instructed leaders dealing with a crisis to quit trying to be Atlas "and get the world off your shoulders."[48] Leaders need to realize they are not in the crisis alone (see Matt 28:19). The stylistic competency of empowering leadership encompasses the *ability to let go and let others*. Leaders do not have to be strong in all of the leadership qualities that are optimum in a crisis. Instead, they must team with others to compensate for any deficiencies. For instance, the primary leader may lack the creativity needed in a crisis. As Kaplan noted, "If you aren't an out-of-the-box thinker, you can recruit one."[49]

The need for empowerment is more than keeping the leader from being overwhelmed. In addition, the previously mentioned axiom "never waste a good crisis" is a reminder to ministry leaders of their ultimate purpose of making disciples. The silver lining of a crisis cloud is its enormous opportunity for developing leaders. In crisis mode, people who have never significantly contributed as leaders may want to help. Others who have been active leaders rise to a new level of effectiveness and demonstrate talents that had been lying dormant. At First Baptist Church Shreveport, Gene Hendrix reflected, "In a situation like this we needed both. We needed people to step up based on their skills and their gifts. And people did that, which I think is indicative of the people of God and how He works in churches." A crisis brings an extra incentive to do what churches should always be doing, "the training of the saints in the work of ministry, to build up the body of Christ" (Eph 4:12).

> *The silver lining of a crisis cloud is its enormous opportunity for developing leaders.*

Empowering leadership requires discernment as to how much can be delegated. A situational leadership model, as advocated by Paul Hersey and Roger Chevalier, is one in which the leader exercises a coaching competency.[50] According to the person's readiness, the leaders make adjustments as to how much or how little direction the person needs. The process is similar to the way a college football coach might work with a new freshman quarterback versus a seasoned senior. Leaders must not underestimate the potential of someone, nor can they afford to overwhelm the new leader. The leader must also discern whether individuals want to take a significant leadership role or are not ready for it. In such cases, forcing them to take a leadership role could be disastrous. As Sashkin and Sashkin posited, "Transformational leaders carefully assess the ability of followers to perform and succeed."[51] There is risk, but it is calculated. The empowering leader must provide the training, resources, and support the new leader needs to succeed.

Despite the best resources and training, leaders must be willing to allow those they empower to fail. They must not pull support at the first evidence of a mistake. No sports team has a deep enough bench to remove everyone from the playing field each time they make a mistake. Neither can the church put on the shelf those who fail. In a crisis, some of the best and most experienced leaders will fail, whereas some of the least experienced will succeed, and vice versa. No guarantees of immediate success exist, but a more important result may occur in the long run. Jesus gave His disciples opportunities for ministry, but He did not set them up for failure or allow them to perish. He allowed Peter to walk on the water but pulled him up when he began to sink. When the disciples failed, Jesus did not give up on them but used the experience as a teachable, transformational moment.

Beyond coping with the actual crisis in the period of its occurrence, empowering leadership helps prepare for the eventuality of a crisis. The normal high demands of leadership are so great that it is hard for leaders to think about or invest energy into preparing for an unanticipated crisis. Yet crises do happen. Leaders must think ahead "to analyze the ability for an organizational environment to respond and cope with the unexpected."[52] Steven Fink admonished that leaders "should view and plan for the inevitability of a crisis in much the same way [one] views and plans for the inevitability of death and taxes; not out of weakness or fear, but out of the strength that comes from knowing you are prepared."[53] By practicing empowering leadership, others are already prepared to step up to the challenge. Fred Winters could never have imagined that he would be taken from his flock in such a tragic manner, but his empowering leadership enabled others to carry on his vision of the transformational mission of the gospel.

Churches are less likely to spend extensive time recruiting or training a crisis response team. However, an enlisted team could engage in simple contingency planning for issues such as: Who will be the spokesperson? How will communication occur? How will they cope with the disruption of the normal flow of decision making, mobilize internal resources, and enlist outside resources? Such a process could prove invaluable and have the bonus benefit of providing a means to teach constituents how servant leaders respond to crises.

Empowering leadership has an important relationship to decisive leadership and empathetic leadership. Being decisive does not negate the value of a team. The author of Prov 24:6 noted, "Victory comes with many counselors." Decisive leaders need the balance of a leadership process with other empowered leaders to build consensus. Empowering leadership is also a natural complement of the empathetic leader or servant leader. Whereas the empathetic or servant leader demonstrates the biblical mode of leadership, empowerment demonstrates the biblical goal of leadership, which is transformation. Whether in the midst of the trial of a difficult crisis or in the normal high demands of leadership, the leader must remember that empowering people from a biblical perspective means to lead them to become fully devoted followers of Christ.

Creative Leadership

> *Creative leadership involves responding with innovation and intuition to find solutions to problems and challenges that cannot be solved through previously established means.*

For his leadership in the greatest financial crisis since the Great Depression, *Time* magazine named Federal Reserve Chairman Ben Bernanke its Person of the Year for 2009. Differing with Bernanke's critics who charged that his policies contributed to the precarious situation, the magazine writers maintained that his response to the crisis averted a financial meltdown. They argued that the gravity of the situation required measures that no one had done before and that "his creative leadership helped ensure that 2009 was a period of weak recovery rather than catastrophic depression."[54] Bernanke said that when "orthodoxy fails, then you need to try new things."[55] The need to try an unorthodox approach is one of the keys to crisis leadership. As Leonard noted, "True crisis situations invalidate the approach of simply activating existing routines or common and practiced combinations of routines."[56] Often leaders cannot solve crisis problems through traditional means but instead may need to think creatively.

> *The search to find the creative solution drives the leader beyond the scripted response.*

The search to find the creative solution drives the leader beyond the scripted response. At this point, intuition is a key in finding creative solutions. Richard Daft noted, "Intuition is not arbitrary or irrational; it is based on years of practice and hands-on experience."[57] Leaders can bring their accumulated experiences and skill sets to the crisis. As a result, a previously successful leader often "can rapidly perceive and understand problems and develop a gut feeling or hunch" about a solution that is not necessarily proven.[58] Sashkin and Sashkin asserted that crafting a creative solution "involves a willingness to take risks."[59]

The distinction for Christian leaders is that they take risks based on faith in God and not solely on their innate or acquired skills. For Christian ministry leaders, the need to find a creative solution should foster an even greater sense of dependence on God. Ed Young observed, "Creativity is immensely difficult and especially taxing on a leader. . . . The pursuit of creativity has driven me to my knees more than any other leadership task."[60] If finding the creative solution is taxing in normal leadership circumstances, it is much more so in the intensity of crisis leadership. Because the new approach is unproven, attempting it takes faith and courage. Ministry leaders find themselves like a modern-day

Joshua. Figuratively, they face the challenge to believe that God can part the Jordan River, bring down the walls of Jericho, and even make the sun stand still! As with Joshua, these divine, outside-the-box, creative solutions that enable God's leaders to solve seemingly intractable problems also require them to "be strong and courageous" (Josh 1:18).

Transformational leaders provide an environment that fosters opportunities for constituents to be creative.[61] Creative leadership has strong connections with the aforementioned leadership competencies. Leaders who communicate the vision in a manner that brings alignment, establishes trust, and empowers followers in such a way that allows risk of failure have a greater chance to see creativity flourish. Solutions to difficult problems by thinking in new ways bring benefits that often far outlast the time of crisis. The creativity that flows forth can perpetuate an ongoing transformation of both the individual and the entire congregation or ministry.

Deploy the Boats!

Leadership is a tough challenge in the best of times. John Gardner reflected, "Acclaim and derision are the rewards of leadership. The laurel is interlaced with poison ivy."[62] Crises intensify this tendency. For the leader, crises are times of unprecedented opportunity for triumph or disaster. Norman R. Augustine observed, "Almost every crisis contains within itself the seeds of success as well as the roots of failure."[63] Crises have a way of revealing the weaknesses of a congregation or ministry organization. If the leader does not address these, the potential for disaster is increased. However, the sense of urgency creates the opportunity to change the congregation or ministry organization in a positive way. Ron Dufresne noted, "Effective crisis leadership is really . . . imagining a future that brings you beyond the status quo."[64] Thus, the seeds of future success lie in the opportunity of the moment of greatest challenge.

Although ministry leaders rarely anticipate a catastrophic crisis, God is never surprised and already has a plan. The supernatural efficacy of the power of God can turn a catastrophic crisis into testimonies of His redeeming grace. He is "a helper who is always found in times of trouble" (Ps 46:1). In His provision, there are always more than enough leadership lifeboats for ministry leaders who will utilize them. Moreover, it is not necessary to repeat the mistakes of the *Titanic* in order to learn from and implement the lessons of the *Titanic*. What ministry leaders learn from their own crises and the crises of others can aid them in navigating the uncertain and sometimes icy waters of future challenges. When a crisis comes, *deploy the leadership lifeboats to the fullest and trust that God will be with you in the voyages ahead.*

Questions for Further Thought

1. In the practice of ministry leadership, what is the difference between a leadership stance and a leadership style?
2. Of the seven stylistic leadership competencies, which do you think is the most likely to be detrimentally overused? Which ones do you think are most often lacking in crises as well as in the normative challenges of leadership? Which ones are you most likely to use or not use when facing a crisis?
3. What synergism have you experienced or observed between any of the competencies?
4. How might personality and giftedness affect the employment of the seven stylistic competencies?
5. How does the presence of a crisis increase the need for balance in employing some of the competencies?
6. What is the distinction between being flexible in utilizing the seven leadership stylistic competencies and being inconsistent?

Notes

1. J. Maxwell, *Developing the Leader in You* (Nashville: Thomas Nelson Publishers, 1993), xi.

2. B. Robert and C. Lajtha, "A New Approach to Crisis Management," *Journal of Contingencies and Crisis Management* (December 2002): 10.4:186.

3. R. D. Dale, *Pastoral Leadership* (Nashville: Abingdon Press, 1986), 34.

4. R. T. Greenleaf, *Servant Leadership: A Journey into the Nature of Legitimate Power and Greatness* (Mahwah, NJ: Paulist Press, 1977), 7.

5. J. M. Burns, *Leadership* (New York: Harper Press, 1978), 4.

6. P. V. Lewis, *Transformational Leadership: A New Model for Total Church Involvement* (Nashville: B&H, 1996), 97.

7. P. T. P. Wong, "An Opponent-Process Model of Servant Leadership and a Typology of Leadership Styles," based on a presentation given at the Servant Leadership Roundtable and the ensuing discussions at Regent University, Virginia Beach, VA, 16 October 2003, 2; available at http://www.twu.ca/academics/graduate/ leadership/servant-leadership/servant-leadership-roundtable-typology.pdf.

8 B. Kaplan (with R. Kaiser), *The Versatile Leader: Make the Most of Your Strengths—Without Overdoing It* (San Francisco: Pfeiffer, 2006), 9.

9. S. S. Sample, *The Contrarian's Guide to Leadership* (San Francisco: Jossey-Bass, 2002), 110.

10. D. Brinkley, *The Great Deluge: Hurricane Katrina, New Orleans, and the Mississippi Gulf Coast* (New York: HarperCollins, 2006), 34.

11. H. Blackaby and R. Blackaby, *Spiritual Leadership: Moving People on to God's Agenda* (Nashville: B&H, 2001), 20.

12. J. O. Sanders, *Spiritual Leadership: Principles of Excellence for Every Believer*, 2nd ed. (Chicago: Moody Press, 1994), 15.

13. M. King, "Widow of Slain Ill. Pastor Points to 'Celebration Day'" *Baptist Press*, March 13, 2009; available from http://www.bpnews.net/bpnews.asp?id=30066 (accessed March 13, 2009).

14. C. Winters, CBS interview, March 28, 2009, posted on Founders Ministries Blog, http://www.founders.org/blog/2009/03/interview-with-cindy-widow-of-pastor.html (accessed April 21, 2010).

15. K. P. Yusko and H. W. Goldstein, "Selecting and Developing Crisis Leaders Using Competency-Based Simulations," *Journal of Contingencies and Crisis Management* 5 (December 1997): 219.

16. J. R. Clinton, *The Making of a Leader: Recognizing the Lessons and Stages of Leadership Development* (Colorado Springs: NavPress, 1988), 164.

17. Brinkley, *The Great Deluge*, 89.

18. W. Weir, *50 Military Leaders Who Changed the World* (New York: Fall River Press, 2007), 51, 153.

19. T. S. Laniak, *Shepherds after My Own Heart: Pastoral Traditions and Leadership in the Bible*, New Studies in Biblical Theology (Downers Grove, IL: InterVarsity Press, 2006), 21.

20. E. Stern, "Crisis Navigation: Lessons from History for the Crisis Manager in Chief," *Governance: An International Journal of Policy, Administration, and Institutions* (April 2009), 22.2:190.

21. J. Kotter, *Leading Change* (Boston: Harvard Business School Press, 1996), 9.

22. I. I. Mitroff with G. Anagos, *Managing Crises before They Happen: What Every Executive and Manager Needs to Know about Crisis Management* (New York: American Management Association, 2001), 55–57.

23. J. M. Kouzes and B. Posner, *Credibility: How Leaders Gain and Lose It, Why People Demand It* (San Francisco: Jossey-Bass, 1991), 14–15.

24. P. Hart, L. Heyse, and A. Boin, "Guest Editorial Introduction: New Trends in Crisis Management Practice and Crisis Management Research:

Setting the Agenda," *Journal of Contingencies and Crisis Management* (December 2001), 9.4:183.

25. D. Goleman, "Leadership That Gets Results," *Harvard Business Review* (March–April 2000): 81.

26. Lewis, *Transformational Leadership*, 93.

27. M. Useem, *The Leadership Moment: Nine True Stories of Triumph and Disaster and Their Lessons for Us All* (New York: Random House, 1998), 4.

28. Stern, "Crisis Navigation," 190.

29. M. Sashkin and M. G. Sashkin, *Leadership That Matters: The Critical Factors for Making a Difference in People's Lives and Organizations' Success* (San Francisco: Berrett-Koehler Publishers, 2003), 2.

30. R. A. Heifetz, *Leadership without Easy Answers* (Cambridge: Belknap Press of Harvard University Press, 2001), 225.

31. Kotter, *Leading Change*, 68.

32. D. A. Garrett, *Proverbs, Ecclesiastes, Song of Solomon*, The New American Commentary, ed. E. R. Clendenen (Nashville: Broadman, 1993), 230.

33. M. Shelley, *Well-Intentioned Dragons: Ministering to Problem People in the Church* (Waco, TX: Word Books, 1985), 83.

34. P. Senge, *The Fifth Discipline: The Art and Practice of the Learning Organization* (New York: Doubleday, 1990), 9.

35. J. Herrington, M. Bonem, and J. H. Furr, *Leading Congregational Change: A Practical Guide for the Transformational Journey* (San Francisco: Jossey-Bass, 2000), 35.

36. G. Yukl, *Leadership in Organizations*, 4th ed. (Upper Saddle River, NJ: Prentice-Hall, 1998), 31.

37. D. Goleman, R. Boyatzis, and A. McKee, *Primal Leadership: Realizing the Power of Emotional Intelligence* (Boston: Harvard Business School Press, 2002), 78.

38. Yukl, *Leadership in Organizations*, 62.

39. Ibid.

40. Sashkin and Sashkin, *Leadership That Matters*, 195.

41. D. R. Caruso and P. Salovey, *The Emotionally Intelligent Manager: How to Develop and Use the Four Key Emotional Skills of Leadership* (San Francisco: Jossey-Bass, 2004), 171.

42. D. Goleman, *Social Intelligence: Beyond IQ, Beyond Emotional Intelligence* (New York: Bantam Dell, 2006), 61–62.

43. R. K. Greenleaf, *Servant Leadership: A Journey into the Nature of Legitimate Power and Greatness* (New York: Paulist Press, 1977), 21.

44. Wong, "An Opponent Process Model," 2.

45. K. Blanchard and P. Hodges, *Lead Like Jesus: Lessons from the Greatest Leadership Role Model of All Time* (Nashville: Word Publishing Group, 2005), 40.

46. Caruso and Salovey, *The Emotionally Intelligent Manager*, 47.

47. D. Bowling and D. A. Hoffman, *Bringing Peace into the Room: How the Personal Qualities of the Mediator Impact the Process of Conflict Resolution* (San Francisco: Jossey-Bass, 2003),160.

48. B. George, *7 Lessons for Leading in Crisis* (San Francisco: Jossey-Bass, 2009), 31.

49. Kaplan, *The Versatile Leader*, 108.

50. P. Hersey and R. Chevalier, "Situational Leadership and Executive Coaching," in *Coaching for Leadership: The Practice of Leadership Coaching from the World's Greatest Coaches*, 2nd ed., ed. M. Goldsmith and L. Lyons (San Francisco: Pfeiffer, 2006), 26.

51. Sashkin and Sashkin, *Leadership That Matters*, 195.

52. C. Smith, C. Jennings, and N. Castro, "Models for Assessing Adaptive Effectiveness Development," *Journal of Contingencies and Crisis Management* 13 (September 2005): 136.

53. N. R. Augustine, "Managing the Crisis You Tried to Prevent," in *Harvard Business Review on Crisis Management* (Boston: Harvard Business School Press, 2000), 11.

54. M. Grunwald, "Ben Bernanke: The 2009 *Time* Person of the Year," *Time*, December 28, 2009–January 4, 2010, 48.

55. Ibid., 78.

56. H. B. Leonard, "Crisis," in *Encyclopedia of Leadership*, ed. G. R. Goethals, G. J. Sorenson, and J. McGregor Burns (Thousand Oaks, CA: Sage Publications), 290.

57. R. L. Daft, *Leadership Theory and Practice* (Fort Worth: Harcourt Brace College Publishers, 1999), 461.

58. Ibid., 462.

59. Sashkin and Sashkin, *Leadership That Matters*, 195.

60. E. Young, *The Creative Leader* (Nashville: B&H, 2006), 22–23.

61. Sashkin and Sashkin, *Leadership That Matters*, 195.

62. J. Gardner, *On Leadership* (New York: Free Press, 1990), 53.

63. Augustine, "Managing the Crisis You Tried to Prevent," 3.

64. B. Schulte, "The Silver Lining of Trouble," *U.S. News and World Report*, November 2009, 24.

Chapter 10

Aftermath: Hope Following the Crisis

"He comforts us in all our affliction, so that we may be able to comfort those who are in any kind of affliction, through the comfort we ourselves receive from God." 2 Corinthians 1:4

We have looked closely at a number of leadership issues in dealing with a catastrophic crisis in its unfolding. Working in the new normal also means dealing with the longer-term aftermath. One overriding aspect of the aftermath that continues for the indefinite future is loss. Some of the case studies in this book involved intense grief over the death of loved ones. Such grief has incomparable pain. All the other normally anticipated issues of ministering to the grieving were present. However, another type of grief resulted from loss of the old normal—the familiar and comforting aspects that would never return. The church or ministry organization must address these needs.

We noted in these case studies that the new normal sometimes brought resistance. Bethel Baptist Church had an element who wanted the "Old Bethel." Chuck Kelley found that resistance to further change was greater than expected. Numerous other examples were evident. In a sense, a catastrophic crisis shatters the status quo. To attempt to return to the old is like trying to reconstruct a vase broken into multiple pieces. Even if you can glue it back together, there is always a missing piece and it never looks the same. However, the shape of the past does influence the future, since the new normal always contains elements of the past. The goal for leadership is not to be limited to the past. To use the vase illustration, God can take the broken pieces of a catastrophic crisis and, with some additional ingredients, recast it into something new. Although this new normal may elicit the memory of the old, it is something beyond the old.

More than looking at these change dynamics exclusively from the larger overview of the congregation or ministry organization as a whole, we must note how a crisis affects specific individuals. By doing so, we lessen the risk of a merely theoretical consideration of leadership ideas. Instead, we deal with the reality of the effects of a crisis on people's lives. It is in this arena that leadership makes the real difference. In this chapter, we take a close look at the experiences of three people. Each one experienced a catastrophic crisis that turned his life upside down. Like the other accounts in the book, these situations provide some leadership lessons. Even more important is the belief that God's grace brings new blessings in the new normal. If the key word for our lifeboat chapter was *help*, our key word here is *hope*.

Personal Experience: Allen England

When I interviewed Chuck Kelley for the case study on NOBTS, he said something that I will always remember: "I have learned the difference between trouble and catastrophe. Trouble is difficulty. Trouble is challenging. Trouble can be painful. Catastrophe changes everything. Trouble comes and then passes. A catastrophic crisis comes and stays." Often we have difficulties that come and never go away. God has taught me this lesson through first-hand experience. Even in the

> *"Trouble comes and then passes. A catastrophic crisis comes and stays."*

writing of this book, I discovered that I was still coping with the lingering effects caused by the trauma of Katrina. Interviewing those who were hurting reopened some of the wounds the crisis had created for my family and me. As I heard their stories, I remembered our experience. These feelings were a reminder that the new normal is not something that we adjust to quickly. Yet, as is evident in my experience as well as the others we have explored, God can meet both our immediate and our continual needs with His provisions and grace.

A week or so after Hurricane Katrina, Kelley called the entire faculty of NOBTS to meet on the campus of Southwestern Baptist Theological Seminary (see chap. 1). The only problem was that many of the faculty (myself included) had lost everything, including our clothes. So there we were back home in Knoxville in a mall getting ready to purchase a large amount of clothes with money that family and friends had given us. Therein lay my problem.

My wife, Jane, was excited at the prospect of getting to see everyone from the seminary and having a new wardrobe as well. I just sat on a bench in the mall, dejected. In reality, I was feeling sorry for myself. Jane asked me why I did not share her enthusiasm. I replied that it is no fun to buy clothes with money I did not earn. My male ego made me feel like a charity case.

Jane looked at me with frustration and reminded me, "Please, don't confuse God's provision with your activity. Regardless of the source of this money, God has provided it. Sometimes He allows you to earn the money that He provides, but this time He has used His people to provide for our needs. Either way God is the One who meets our needs, not you!" Then she gave the stinger, *"So get over yourself!"* I thank God for Jane! I got up and enjoyed the day with my godly bride!

Everyone experiences hurricanes in life. Sometimes they really are hurricanes, but most of the time they are just the circumstances of our lives that have gone awry. Crises happen to us all. Sometimes we bring a crisis on ourselves. At times, however, we are truly innocent victims wounded by a crisis. We can react poorly, as I did, and thereby worsen the event. In the end, the way we respond to a crisis makes all the difference.

Almost every course I teach at the seminary directly or indirectly concerns church leadership and administration. Accordingly, I believe and teach that the proper use of policies and organizational structure will provide a foundation for an enhanced ministry in the local church. However, I hasten to add that there are some things for which we cannot plan. When a catastrophic crisis occurs, usually there is no policy to follow or structure strong enough to contain the crisis. The case studies in this book corroborate this truism. Even so, the way we as leaders respond to a crisis on a personal level will have great impact not only on the recovery of the group we lead but on ourselves as well. Our response has the potential to calm or worsen a crisis. I have Prov 3:5–8 written in the front of my Bible as a reminder that sometimes I cannot trust my own judgment.

Consider the following case study of Ron Cherry. Here we find a devoted man of God whose response to the crisis in which he found himself was a key to overcoming it. Through God's redemption, Ron received a new direction that ultimately led him to a new normal.

Ron Cherry's Story

My train ran off the rail because I kept thinking as soon as I finish this deal, this crisis, this goal, this program I will go back and give attention to what I should be giving attention to all along. I taught people that they were supposed to love their wives as Christ loved the church. I knew all that stuff. Nobody could counsel me because I knew it better than they did. It was a matter of taking the time to put it into practice in my life. So, eventually I just said you know what, "I am going to lose my ministry, I am going to lose my family and my life. It is going to be gone from me if I just do not do the right things. I will not worry about the results; I will put it all in God's hands." Ron Cherry

Ron and Kay had been married for 10 years and had two wonderful children. Both Ron and Kay loved Jesus, both felt called into ministry, and both loved each other and their family. Ron had started preaching when he was 15 years old. He had served in multiple pastorates for 15 years, and God had blessed him with highly successful ministries. He recently left a large downtown church in Plant City, Florida, to start a church in Plano, Texas. Everything in Ron's life seemed to be going very well.

"I will tell you what an awful lot of guys that I had counseled told me: I was absolutely shocked when I came home and found that Kay had left, taken the kids and filed for divorce!" recounted Ron. In terms of his initial knowledge of the events, he really did not know his marriage was in trouble. He knew Kay was not happy, but neither Ron nor Kay had ever bought into the notion of marriage being a disposable relationship. They both had a deep conviction that marriage is a commitment before God between a man and a woman for a lifetime. Consequently, he was completely shocked. He had no knowledge of where Kay and the children were.

After Ron collected himself, he picked up the phone and called his chairman of deacons. Ron attempted to explain the events that surrounded his family and what had occurred. The chairman of deacons graciously responded by encouraging Ron to take a sabbatical or some other form of extended time away from the church. Ron answered, "I don't think that I am going to be able to work this out in two weeks or two months or something like that, and I don't want to put the

> *"I have to go find my family and win them back."*

church through those difficulties so I am just resigning." Ron went on to say that he hated to leave the church that way, but, in Ron's words, "I have to go find my family and win them back."

Ron did not know how to do it. He just decided to try to restore his marriage. Everybody they knew—all of their friends, her family—told him to forget it, that she did not want anything to do with him. However, Ron pursued Kay, and after six months they started working things out. Ron and Kay went to several Christian counselors, and even the Christian counselors told them their problems were too extensive to overcome. However, Ron decided that this advice was not sound. He had missed God's will before, and he refused to give up on their marriage. Ron remembers, "I'll do the right thing whether I feel like it or not. I know

God's Word is good and I will get the right results." Ron tried desperately to convince Kay that restoring their relationship was indeed his intention.

Ron was operating on the *cognitive* understanding that his first obligation was to his family, even before his pastoral ministry in the church. However, after he was able to grasp the situation and better formalize his thoughts, he realized that he had not always lived out this priority in his life. Clearly, the Lord had blessed him with great ability to lead the people of God and the organizations within the church; in fact, most of the churches in which he had been the pastor had doubled, tripled, and even quadrupled. He knew how to motivate people and how to place them in the most strategically advantageous areas in the ministries of the church. Even so, until then he had failed to apply many of these same principles in his own family. The reality of his failure to notice this inconsistency in his life hit him like a ton of bricks. Ron wondered, "What did I do here? How can this be?"

As Ron began to comprehend the weight of the episode, he realized that not only was he losing his wife and children, which was almost more than he could bear, but in many ways he was losing his identity as well. He began to realize that the self-image of a man who serves as a pastor becomes *pastor*—this was his identity, and for Ron now this also was in great jeopardy. As Ron explained it, "All of my education was in ministry, all my contacts were in ministry, all my friends were in ministry, everybody I knew, my whole life, my self image, everything was tied up in my identity as pastor and suddenly it was just gone!"

Based on nothing but the belief that it was wrong to be divorced, wrong for their children, and a wrong testimony, Ron and Kay decided to get back together. They agreed to tough it out even if it meant hating each other for the rest of their lives. However, they shared the premise that if they did the right things, eventually they would feel the right feelings. They got together after about six months and started to work on their marriage. That is when Ron embraced the reality that his identity was no longer a pastor. He had to put it aside. Instead, he put all his energy into rebuilding his family. He started to read the Bible with his family in mind. He had never really done that before. Ron asked himself, "How do I lead my family? What are the principles of leadership I have to exert?" He decided he would find out what biblical leadership for the family was all about and attempted to translate these issues into a doable list. Ron realized he had a Type A personality. He did not come across as a sweet, humble guy. He did not intend to be intimidating or arrogant, but sometimes that was what he communicated. Ron turned his attention to the biblical admonition, "The greatest among you will be your servant" (Matt 23:11). Ron tried to find ways to make service his top priority.

After Ron and his wife were together for a few months, he went into the commercial real estate business. He thought he would get back into ministry eventually. However, the church was not receptive to his returning. When a man has had marital problems, even when resolved, the church feels there is a risk involved. The church does not want to give such a high-profile position to a man who has had a meltdown with his family because it may happen again.

Ron also discovered when the word got out about his family problems that all his friends, all his associates, all the people with whom he worked just vaporized. All but one man turned away from him. His identity as a pastor was gone. The way he saw himself—all his goals, all his education, all his preparation for life—everything disappeared. Ron came face to face with the truth that a man's vocation severely impacts his identity, particularly for a pastor. Again, Ron asked himself, "What am I going to do? How do I make a living? How do I see myself? Am I always going to be second best?" Kay also wondered, "What do you do when your life doesn't turn out the way you thought it would?" Similarly, Ron pondered the question, "Are you always David who did not get to build the temple the way you wanted?"

One of the things Ron learned is the mistake multiplier in the life of a pastor. Jesus said, "Much will be required of everyone who has been given much" (Luke 12:48). Pastors are supposed to operate on a higher level of responsibility and obligation. Yet sometimes a pastor can do unwise things that disqualify him for ministry. Ron determined that he had too much respect for the ministry to go back. Another vocation was necessary. He had to form a new identity. Years later Ron attempted to do staff ministry at a large church only to realize those doors had been closed forever. Even so, the Lord blessed Ron in his business ventures and made a way for him to secure a new identity as a Christian layman.

Beyond the Story: Leadership Lessons from Ron

Ron had always been a very driven personality. He was a doer. No one had told him the importance of knowing his personality type and its potential effect on his ministry. Ron associated his personality type with his calling. In addition, he did not know which spiritual gifts the Holy Spirit had given him. As a result, Ron began his ministry as a very confused pastor. Without understanding some important things about himself, Ron had plunged into ministry headfirst. He falsely believed that because he was the pastor, he must possess *every* spiritual gift and do all the work of the church.

He began to feel the church encouraging him to do all and be all in the church. He did not allow the laity to fulfill their own roles because he thought he could do them better. He delegated to the laity only when doing so enhanced church growth. Ron was not trying to exclude the people of God from their called responsibilities. He was working out his ministry in all sincerity. Yet Ron had become a results-oriented, perfectionist workaholic. The pressure to perform was enormous, but Ron thrived on the challenge. He coped by working harder. His goal was always bigger, better, greater—always improving. Looking back, Ron recounted how the Scripture commands that ministers must equip the laity for the work of ministry. "The bottom line is I was trying to do all the right things, but I failed miserably," Ron recalled.

> *Without understanding some important things about himself, Ron had plunged into ministry headfirst. He falsely believed that because he was the pastor, he must possess every spiritual gift and do all the work of the church.*

The performance into which Ron had fallen did not stop with his ministry at church but was present at home as well. He wanted Kay to rear their children all by herself. After all, he was providing a nice home, private schools for the kids, a car that did not break down. Ron falsely deduced that he had communicated his love and commitment to his family by providing their material needs and desires and giving them whatever time remained. "I thought she would recognize that I loved her because I came home every night, and I was not going to the bar." He was killing himself. Did Kay not know that he loved her? He reasoned that she enjoyed the prestige of being the pastor's wife. She had a lot of friends and a good lifestyle. The only problem was that Kay did not see things that way. As Ron later reflected, he saw that he did not treat Kay in the manner that Christ treated the church. He provided material goods for her, but she viewed those things as products of his doing things for the church, not directly for her.

Kay and their children had become a resource in Ron's life. Leadership and management are not synonyms. Management is about control—controlling the resources of the organization toward the achievement of its goals. Although management is clearly necessary, few people enjoy being managed. He had expected Kay to fall in line with their life's circumstances and be just as happy as he was while he worked away from home 80 hours a week. He thought her responsibility was to create beauty and nurture. What Ron did not understand was that their roles had to be in harmony, and he did not provide a vision to bring her alongside him. He did not perceive anything she was trying to say. They were talking different languages. Ron did not realize he was managing Kay by treating her as a subordinate rather than leading in a biblical manner. Leadership is based on trust. One must take the time to invest and build relationships with others to gain the right to lead. He failed to recognize the partnership they shared as husband and wife as well as the talents and gifts she brought to their marriage.

Although Ron did not set out to devalue his family, he allowed the busyness of the ministry to overshadow his family. This busyness caused him to lose sight of his first calling, which was to lead and nurture his wife and children. Focusing on the immediacy of the work of the church took priority over his spiritual life. Unintentionally, Ron had replaced his wife and children with the white noise of ministry. He had become emotionally detached from his family. Ron recalled, "I let the doing of good things to become the tool that Satan used to take me out of the work. The very thing I loved became the thing that competed with my wife, and she saw it as a mistress."

When Ron and Kay married, Ron never thought about what marriage was supposed to be like. "I had just fallen in love with her, married her, and figured it would all work out." He failed to spend time learning about Kay and trying to understand her. He repeated this failure with his children. Ron did not understand the essentiality of communication in a relationship. Consequently, Kay felt left out and minimized. Although living under the same roof, Kay did not feel she shared a life with Ron.

Communication was also an issue in Ron's ministry. Ron was the type of person who, even when he counseled and during his pastoral ministry, would tell the person what the Bible said and then end the session without any further interaction. When he dealt with his staff, he would outline the plan and instructions and then expect them to go do it. If they came back to ask for further instruction, he would say he had nothing else to talk about. He would tell them to go back and figure it out. Although Ron was a great pulpit speaker, he was a very poor communicator one on one. Communicating did not come naturally to him. He did not realize communication was a key in building a team.

Retooling for Leadership

God used the crisis in Ron's life to get his attention. After Kay and the children moved back in with Ron, he began to work on family relationships and how to lead his family. The Holy Spirit gave Ron biblical leadership principles for his family, and Ron began to translate these principles into actions.

- Ron recognized that his Type A personality caused some folks to see him as intimidating. He did not intend to come across that way, but he did. Ron made it a priority to reconfigure the strengths of his personality to serve his family. Ron recalled with determination, "I said

> *God used the crisis in Ron's life to get his attention.*

to myself, I am going to show my family that they are first. I am going to find ways to do that, so that became my primary goal."

- Ron had seen his family collapse because of a lack of vision. Through the Scriptures, he determined what the new vision for his family would be. In order for their family to develop intimacy, he needed to lead by example by allowing access and availability. Ron needed to be present and approachable. Kay needed the freedom and opportunity to share her vision, her thoughts, and her abilities. This marriage needed to be a partnership.

- Ron recognized he was an emotionally detached individual and that showing emotion was difficult for him. Ron operated out of a system of logic and rationale. It was difficult for Ron to become emotionally vulnerable to Kay and the children, but he determined that this was a primary goal from Scripture. Although today he still struggles with emotional intimacy and it does not come naturally to him, he has worked at being approachable and transparent.

- Ron determined he needed to develop an ability to communicate with his family until he knew they understood his priorities. This task was difficult, as Ron was not used to including his family. His wife was not used to Ron taking her seriously. Ron's priority was to become a great one-on-one communicator with his family and others. Ironically, greater ability to communicate has made Ron much more successful in his business endeavors.

New Direction and a New Normal

God allowed Ron to win back his family. The Lord used this crisis to bring a great benefit in the lives of Ron, Kay, and their children. At the time of these events, the children were too young to see or understand the real struggle the family faced. The children received the greatest benefit since the crisis forced Ron to seek biblical guidance and direction for leading his family. Ron reminisced, "Because of my search for finding biblical truth, we have a great family and are very close today." Thirty years later, Ron and Kay are deeply involved in their children's lives in a healthy fashion.

When Ron was a pastor, he asked his congregation whether they could run their business as a ministry, being honest and forthright. Now that he was in business, Ron wondered whether he could pass the test. Would he be just as honest and forthright and use his business as a ministry opportunity to tell others about Jesus? God continues to bless Ron with success in his business endeavors because his primary goal is to honor God in his business rather than to focus on prestige, power, and financial gain. Ron asked himself, "What does the Bible say about this situation? How can I do it?" These questions became the watchwords for his life, and his family has embraced them as well. The first question Ron asks a client is, "What is the right thing to do in this situation?"

Ron's success in business does not replace the pain of losing his ministry. To this day, he and Kay continue to grieve over the loss of his pastoral ministry. "I was a failure at being what God called me to be: a pastor, a pastoral preacher. I lost that opportunity, but I was not a failure at raising my children, which should have been my primary goal. I should have gotten that right to begin with, and I could have done them both. But I didn't and I had to end up making a choice." Ron put his desire to preach behind and determined to be the right kind of husband and father before he considered ministry. Although Ron tried to reenter the ministry through a staff position, he realized his time had passed. Even though the disappointment of the loss of his ministry is profound, Ron is encouraged with the knowledge that his own children have healthy, godly families and vibrant ministries of their own.

Ron and Kay decided to allow God to use their struggles in their ministry and marriage to help others who are walking through the same experience. The Lord continues to recycle their pain and grief by helping others see the danger of not doing God's business God's way. Through their personal reconciliation, God has given Ron and Kay a ministry of reconciliation for others.

When the ministry opportunities that God's servant loves so much are removed, even temporarily, the minister faces a great test of faith. Rickey Brantley experienced such a test. While Ron needed to redefine his life because of his own shortcomings, Rickey had no choice but to do so for a very different reason.

Rickey Brantley: Finding Grace for the "Thorn in the Flesh"

"But He said to me, 'My grace is sufficient for you.'"
2 Corinthians 12:9

Rickey Brantley was enjoying his ministry to the fullest. It had been hard to leave Lawrence Baptist Church in Macon, Georgia, where he had been the pastor for almost 18 years. The ministry there had been fruitful and fulfilling. Even at age 47, he felt he could have stayed until retirement. Yet the call was unmistakable to become the pastor of Zion Baptist Church (ZBC) in Covington, Georgia. The transition from a medium-sized city to the Atlanta metropolitan suburb of Covington was challenging, but it went extremely well. The congregation grew by 100 new members the first year. The growth pattern would continue for five years as the church eventually reached over 650 in worship attendance, the highest in its history. Of that time, Rickey said, "I was probably happier and more content in my ministry and my personal life than I had ever been."

The congregation at ZBC was delighted with Rickey's ministry for several reasons. Rickey was the epitome of a caring pastor and servant leader. He made everyone feel special and extended himself to his limits in giving personal pastoral care. In addition, Rickey was a powerful expositor of the Scriptures, regularly preaching through entire books of the Bible. The previous pastor had a solid ministry of 25 years. With effective leadership, Rickey built on that foundation.

One of the reasons Rickey enjoyed the ministry at ZBC was that the church's proximity to the North Georgia Campus of the New Orleans Baptist Theological Seminary allowed him some teaching opportunities. He was highly skilled in the biblical languages, especially Hebrew, which had been the focus of his doctoral work. His students expressed great appreciation for his ability to teach Hebrew in an understandable way. Rickey often gave revealing word pictures that his class members could teach and apply in their ministries. He took this same skill into the pulpit, and his congregation responded with enthusiastic affirmation to his messages. Yet this ideal combination of congregational and seminary ministry was under threat even before Rickey arrived at ZBC.

The threat to Rickey's ministry was not something inside or outside the congregation, nor was it from his spiritual life. The threat to his dream ministry was inside his physical body. Ten years prior to coming to ZBC, Rickey discovered that he had diabetes. The doctors found it through an investigation of the symptoms of pain and numbness in his legs known as neuropathy. At first, medication helped manage his diabetes. However, as the diabetes grew worse, so did the neuropathy. By the time he became pastor at Zion Baptist Church, the pain was becoming more severe. Over the course of time, Rickey developed a high threshold for pain. However, now it was at a new level of intensity. Looking back, he recalled, "I can best describe the pain as feeling like a Volkswagen or a bus is standing [or] sitting on your foot. Some days it was a Volkswagen. Some days it was a bus. . . . At the same time there was a nail, a huge nail, sticking through your foot and all the time your feet were on fire, just blazing fire."

Rickey was reluctant to say anything about the pain to anyone in the church, yet it was becoming more obvious to everyone. Much of his reaction was unconscious. In response to the pain, he once broke the steering wheel of his car while driving. A trip to the dentist revealed that he had chipped or destroyed 14 teeth by grinding them in pain. Finally unable to bear it any longer, Rickey told his endocrinologist how severe the pain had become. A trip to a pain specialist brought Rickey to a point he had hoped would never come. The specialist told Rickey that his only relief would come through narcotics. Reluctantly, but with no choice, Rickey began a regimen of some very powerful narcotics including morphine, oxycodone, and methadone.

From the beginning, Rickey had been open with the church about his diabetic condition. They knew of it when they called him. When he went on narcotics, he likewise told them. Through the difficult mental and physical side effects of the narcotics, the congregation demonstrated understanding. On numerous occasions, the church had special prayer for their pastor. Several times during worship services, men came forward and laid hands on Rickey as they prayed. Every deacons' meeting ended in a similar emphasis on prayer. One member even came and asked permission to anoint Rickey with oil, to which Rickey agreed. The fervency of the prayer was intense. Rickey could identify with Paul and his "thorn in the flesh" that Paul "pleaded with the Lord three times" to remove (2 Cor 12:7–8). Like Paul, Rickey did not have the thorn removed but did find that God's grace was "sufficient" (2 Cor 12:9).

In addition to prayer, the church was supportive in other ways. During his fifth year at the church, a specialized and very extensive surgery at a hospital in Virginia became necessary. The church was so generous with financial help that Rickey was not able to keep an account of how much they gave. "I don't know how much money I had people hand me," he recalled. As the church reached record attendance, somehow Rickey had kept it all going. However, with Rickey's surgery, it was apparent that he needed help. Many came forward to assist. Rickey noted that a number of those who helped had never been involved in ministry or in a leadership position before. The former pastor had been a strong supporter of Rickey's ministry from the beginning. He, along with the staff and the new volunteers, dedicated themselves to meeting the ministry needs of the church.

Despite the strong support to assist Rickey, a few members began to leave. Growth leveled off, and attendance slowly began to slip. No one was pressuring Rickey. In fact, the opposite was true. Leadership in the church constantly approached the pastor to ask what they could do. Rickey began to realize that unless he saw a dramatic change in his health, he would have to step aside. Fortunately, through determination, pain management efforts, and above all God's grace, he eventually was able to move to milder pain medication. Yet his physical condition was simply not good enough to continue to pastor ZBC. After seven years as pastor, despite the protests of the leadership, Rickey felt strongly that the Lord told him it was "time to hang it up for awhile." The church graciously gave him a severance of six months. The leadership offered an even longer severance package, but Rickey refused. The church had done so much that he felt that he could not accept any additional help. He wanted to leave the church as healthy as possible so they could build on the strong foundation that he and others had developed.

Beyond the Story: Leadership Lessons from Rickey

The Importance of Developing Leaders through Modeling

Zion Baptist Church was healthy when Rickey arrived. Rickey's vibrant ministry continued to strengthen the congregation. In addition, the congregation stepped up to face his health crisis so that the church was even stronger at the time Rickey left. God used Rickey's health crisis to develop new leadership. Nonetheless, after Rickey left, the congregation had to work through a grieving process. A good interim and an extended time of more than two years before the next pastor came gave the church time for healing. The new pastor arrived at a church that was in a strong position to move forward.

ZBC is a reminder that church health is the key to surviving and even thriving when a catastrophic crisis comes. The empowering leadership style of the previous pastor and Rickey provided a basis for new leaders to emerge at a critical moment. The spiritual vitality of the pastor was essential. Rickey never felt he was entitled to special treatment and did not want to set himself "above the people." This humility made his congregation desire to minister to him and team with him even more.

Ultimately, the membership of ZBC ministered to Rickey in the manner of the empathetic leadership style that he had modeled before them. His servant ministry had a transformational effect. Rickey's health crisis reminded the congregation that they must accept responsibility for ministry and continually develop new leadership. For various reasons and in various ways, God may remove particular workers from places of service in His kingdom at any time. In order to allow the work to go on, the church must continue to remember its transformational mission and to be diligent in the discipleship process.

New Directions

Rickey found that the transition to leave the pastorate was not an easy one. He missed ministering to people and preaching regularly. His wife, Elaine, had loved being a pastor's wife, but the transition for her was not as difficult. However, she noticed the identity crisis that he was going through. Like ZBC, Rickey had to work through a grieving process. In recalling his feelings, he insisted that he "was no hero." Some dark days came in struggling with the loss, but he did not blame God. He readily admitted that if he had been more diligent in taking care of his physical health, then the complications of his diabetes may have been less severe. In response to his circumstances, Rickey and Elaine moved close to his hometown to be near their daughter and grandchild. Their presence helped with the transition.

Rickey continued to teach in a reduced capacity for the seminary and occasionally serve as a supply preacher while seeking to regain his health. Unfortunately, two years after he resigned from ZBC, he contracted a severe case of the flu. The resulting complications brought a hospital stay of more than two months. Several times during this period, the doctors expressed concern as to whether he would survive. But God intervened. Through the constant care and diligence of Elaine, God guided him to the exact treatment that he needed. After additional time in an extended-care unit and home health service, slowly Rickey's health began to improve.

Through all his struggles with physical infirmities, Rickey declares that his faith has grown immensely. He could not answer all the "imponderables of God's will," but he noted what he had always preached about trusting God came home to be a reality in his own life. The journey since he left ZBC has not been without blessings. Rickey observed, "I have had a lot of time to think and read the Scriptures, and I have never been so excited about the Bible." He sees God's grace in all the support of his former church and his many friends. Not only did he receive continued help from ZBC, but also his previous church in Macon, Lawrence Drive Baptist Church, collected a $10,000 love offering to help with the expenses of his extended hospital stay. He gave God the credit for the rapid approval of his disability support. He is especially grateful for his devoted wife, who has "been my doctor, my friend, my nurse, and anything else you can think of." Rickey has not given up hope in becoming able to pastor again, perhaps at a smaller church. Regardless of the doors that may open or close, Rickey believes that God will use the testimony of the sufficiency of His grace in the midst of the trials he experienced. Though he is not sure of what new directions God may have for him, by faith he is confident that God has a plan for his future ministry.

The Ongoing Journey of Faith: Allen England

The test results came back today and confirmed that my wife has breast cancer. I learned this news only a couple of hours ago. I have no knowledge of the extent or the future outcome. Jane and I had just gotten to a point of making sense out of Hurricane Katrina and the total loss that it caused in the life of our family—and now this.

What do you do when your life spins out of control? How do you find solid ground when you feel like you are constantly rocking back and forth in a boat on a turbulent sea? Where can we go but to the Lord? The "peace of God, which surpasses every thought" (Phil 4:7) is real. None of us knows what tomorrow holds. We can plan and dream, yet our expectations can all come crashing down with a storm, an earthquake, a flat tire, or a visit to the doctor. Eventually we have to come to the point of realizing that what we do as leaders is to invest in people with the hope that they will invest in others as well. That is the cycle of transformational-servant leadership. We continue to lead by investing in a future over which we have minimal control. We may think we have control, but eventually we all realize we do not. That is a key lesson of crisis leadership. In God's sovereignty, He somehow lets us use everything we have learned through our difficulties to make an impact on others at just the right moment. Those we touch then make a difference for the kingdom in God's appointed times. Our responsibility is to be always available, for He is always working. As one of our crisis victims was reminded, "When you cannot trace His hand, that's when you must learn to trust His heart."[1]

Questions for Further Thought

1. Should Ron have resigned his church immediately or should he have followed his deacon chairman's advice and taken a leave of absence? What were the risks and issues for the church and for Ron? Do you think Ron's abrupt resignation is a good pattern to follow in order to make the restoration of the minister's family a priority?

2. Was Ron's leadership style a greater risk for producing the imbalance that resulted in the collapse of his marriage? How could an understanding and practice of the biblical stances of transformational and servant leadership help in keeping the home life healthy?

3. What are some factors that can cause the trauma of a catastrophic crisis to linger? How can they affect the leader's ability to lead?

4. What would have been the pros and cons of Rickey not resigning his pastorate but continuing for a longer period of ministry?

5. How can leaders who have great gifts be consoled when they lose their opportunities to utilize those gifts? Specifically, what would you say to Ron and Rickey?

6. Beyond the particular experiences of Ron, Allen, and Rickey, what are the various ways that all leaders eventually must deal with loss? As a result, what type of grief experiences may or may not occur? How have your own grief experiences affected your manner of leading?

Note

1. F. Cox, *Trusting God's Heart: Finding Peace in Times of Sorrow* (Friendswood, TX: Baxter Press, 2000), 126–27.

Further Resources: Works Cited

Books

Arndt, William F., and F. Wilbur Gingrich. *A Greek-English Lexicon of the New Testament and Other Early Christian Literature*. Chicago: University of Chicago Press, 1957.

Augustine, Norman R. "Managing the Crisis You Tried to Prevent." Pages 1–31 in *Harvard Business Review on Crisis Management*. Boston: Harvard Business School Publishing, 2000.

Banks, Robert, and Bernice Ledbetter. *Reviewing Leadership: A Christian Evaluation of Current Approaches*. Grand Rapids: Baker, 2004.

Blackaby, Henry, and Richard Blackaby. *Spiritual Leadership: Moving People on to God's Agenda*. Nashville: B&H, 2001.

Blanchard, Ken, and Phil Hodges. *Lead Like Jesus: Lessons from the Greatest Leadership Role Model of All Time*. Nashville: Word Publishing Group, 2005.

Bowling, D., and D. A. Hoffman. *Bringing Peace into the Room: How the Personal Qualities of the Mediator Impact the Process of Conflict Resolution*. San Francisco: Jossey-Bass, 2003.

Brinkley, Doug. *The Great Deluge: Hurricane Katrina, New Orleans, and the Mississippi Gulf Coast*. New York: HarperCollins, 2006.

Burns, James McGregor. *Leadership*. New York: Harper Press, 1978.

Caruso, David R., and Peter Salovey. *The Emotionally Intelligent Manager: How to Develop and Use the Four Key Emotional Skills of Leadership.* San Francisco: Jossey-Bass, 2004.

Clinton, J. Robert. *The Making of a Leader: Recognizing the Lessons and Stages of Leadership Development.* Colorado Springs: NavPress, 1988.

Conner, Daryl R. *Managing at the Speed of Change: How Resilient Managers Succeed and Prosper Where Others Fail.* New York: Villard Books, 1992.

Cox, Frank. *Trusting God's Heart: Finding Peace in Times of Sorrow.* Friendswood, TX: Baxter Press, 2000.

Daft, Richard L. *Leadership Theory and Practice.* Fort Worth: Harcourt Brace College Publishers, 1999.

Dale, Robert D. *Pastoral Leadership.* Nashville: Abingdon Press, 1986.

Gardner, J. *On Leadership.* New York: Free Press, 1990.

Garrett, D. A. "Proverbs, Ecclesiastes, Song of Solomon." In *The New American Commentary.* Edited by E. Ray Clendenen. Nashville: Broadman Press, 1993.

George, B. *7 Lessons for Leading in Crisis.* San Francisco: Jossey-Bass, 2009.

Goleman, Daniel. *Social Intelligence: Beyond IQ, Beyond Emotional Intelligence.* New York: Bantam Dell, 2006.

Goleman, Daniel, Richard Boyatzis, and Annie McKee. *Primal Leadership: Realizing the Power of Emotional Intelligence.* Boston: Harvard Business School Press, 2002.

Greenleaf, Robert T. *Servant Leadership: A Journey into the Nature of Legitimate Power and Greatness.* Mahwah, NJ: Paulist Press, 1977.

Heifetz, Ronald A. *Leadership without Easy Answers.* Cambridge: Belknap Press of Harvard University Press, 2001.

Herrington, Jim, Mike Bonem, and James H. Furr. *Leading Congregational Change: A Practical Guide for the Transformational Journey.* San Francisco: Jossey-Bass, 2000.

Hersey, Paul, and Roger Chevalier. "Situational Leadership and Executive Coaching." Pages 26–36 in *Coaching for Leadership: The Practice of Leadership Coaching from the World's Greatest Coaches.* 2d ed. Edited by M. Goldsmith and L. Lyons. San Francisco: Pfeiffer, 2006.

Kaplan, Bob (with Rob Kaiser). *The Versatile Leader: Make the Most of Your Strengths—Without Overdoing It*. San Francisco: Pfeiffer, 2006.

Kotter, John. *Leading Change*. Boston: Harvard Business School Press, 1996.

Kouzes, James M., and Barry Posner. *Credibility: How Leaders Gain and Lose It, Why People Demand It*. San Francisco: Jossey-Bass, 1991.

Laniak, T. S. *Shepherds after My Own Heart: Pastoral Traditions and Leadership in the Bible*. New Studies in Biblical Theology. Downers Grove: InterVarsity Press, 2006.

Leonard, Herman B. "Crisis." Pages 289–95 in *Encyclopedia of Leadership*. Vol. 1. Edited by G. R. Goethals, G. J. Sorenson, and J. McGregor Burns. Thousand Oaks, CA: Sage Publications, 2004.

Lewis, Phillip V. *Transformational Leadership: A New Model for Total Church Involvement*. Nashville: B&H, 1996.

Malphurs, Aubrey. *Being Leaders: The Nature of Authentic Christian Leadership*. Grand Rapids: Baker, 2003.

Maxwell, John. *Developing the Leader in You*. Nashville: Thomas Nelson Publishers, 1993.

Mitroff, Ian I. (with G. Anagos). *Managing Crises before They Happen: What Every Executive and Manager Needs to Know about Crisis Management*. New York: American Management Association, 2001.

Sample, Steven S. *The Contrarian's Guide to Leadership*. San Francisco: Jossey-Bass, 2002.

Sanders, J. Oswald. *Spiritual Leadership: Principles of Excellence for Every Believer*. 2d ed. Chicago: Moody Press, 1994.

Sashkin, Marshall, and Molly G. Sashkin. *Leadership That Matters: The Critical Factors for Making a Difference in People's Lives and Organizations' Success*. San Francisco: Berrett-Koehler Publishers, 2003.

Senge, Peter. *The Fifth Discipline: The Art and Practice of the Learning Organization*. New York: Doubleday, 1990.

Shelley, Marshall. *Well-Intentioned Dragons: Ministering to Problem People in the Church*. Waco, TX: Word Books, 1985.

Useem, Michael. *The Leadership Moment: Nine True Stories of Triumph and Disaster and Their Lessons for Us All*. New York: Random House, 1998.

Weir, William. *50 Military Leaders Who Changed the World*. New York: Fall River Press, 2007.

Young, Ed. *The Creative Leader*. Nashville: B&H, 2006.

Yukl, Gary. *Leadership in Organizations*. 4th ed. Upper Saddle River, NJ: Prentice-Hall, 1998.

Articles

Goleman, Daniel. "Leadership That Gets Results." *Harvard Business Review*, March–April 2000: 78–90.

Grunwald, Michael. "Ben Bernanke: The 2009 *Time* Person of the Year." *Time*, December 28, 2009–January 4, 2010: 44–70.

Hart, Paul T., Liesbet Heyse, and Argen Boin. "Guest Editorial Introduction: New Trends in Crisis Management Practice and Crisis Management Research: Setting the Agenda." *Journal of Contingencies and Crisis Management* 9 (December 2001): 4:181–88.

McQuaid, J., and M. Schleifstein. "The Big One." *The Times-Picayune*, June 24, 2002: A1, A7.

————. "Washing Away." *The Times-Picayune*, June 23, 2002: J2.

Myers, Gary. "As Floodwater Rose at Seminary, Crew Faced Mounting Crisis." *Baptist Press*, September 15, 2005.

Roach, E., M. King, and L. Sergent. *Baptist Press* and the *Illinois Baptist* news journal, March 9 and 10, 2009.

Robert, Bertrand., and Chris Lajtha. "A New Approach to Crisis Management." *Journal of Contingencies and Crisis Management* 10 (December 2002): 4:181–91.

Schulte, Bert. "The Silver Lining of Trouble." *U.S. News and World Report* (November 2009): 24–25.

Smith, Brien N., Ray V. Montagno, and Taitana N. Kuzmenko. "Transformational and Servant Leadership: Content and Contextual Comparisons." *Journal of Leadership and Organizational Studies* 22 (March 2004): 1–3. Accessed at http://leadershipcenter.osu.edu/library/publications/leadership-discoveries/2004/december-2004-transformational-and-servant-leadership-content-and-contextual-comparisons.

Smith, Charlene, Claretha Jennings, and Nancy Castro. "Models for Assessing Adaptive Effectiveness Development." *Journal of Contingencies and Crisis Management* 13 (September 2005): 129–37.

Stern, Eric. "Crisis Navigation: Lessons from History for the Crisis Manager in Chief." *Governance: An International Journal of Policy, Administration, and Institutions* 22 (April 2009): 2:189–202.

Yusko, Kenneth. P., and Harold W. Goldstein. "Selecting and Developing Crisis Leaders Using Competency-Based Simulations." *Journal of Contingencies and Crisis Management* 5 (December 1997): 216–23.

Electronic Sources

Harrison, P. "Never Waste a Good Crisis, Clinton Says on Climate." *Reuters Online*, March 7, 2009. http://in.reuters.com/article/environmentNews/idINTRE5251VN20090306 (accessed December 22, 2009).

King, Martin. "Widow of Slain Ill. Pastor Points to Celebration Day." *Baptist Press*, March 13, 2009. http://www.bpnews.net/bpnews.asp?id=30066 (accessed March 13, 2009).

Winters, Cindy. CBS Interview, March 28, 2009. Posted on Founders Ministries Blog. http://www.founders.org/blog/2009/03/interview-with-cindy-widow-of-pastor.html (accessed April 21, 2010).

Wong, Paul T. P. "An Opponent-Process Model of Servant Leadership and a Typology of Leadership Styles." Based on a presentation given at the Servant Leadership Roundtable and the ensuing discussions at Regent University, Virginia Beach, VA, October 16, 2003. http://www.twu.ca/academics/graduate/leadership/servant-leadership/servant-leadership-roundtable-typology.pdf. (accessed November, 2009).

Name Index

Subject Index

Scripture Index